Virginia's Executive Mansion

Virginia's Executive Mansion

A History of the Governor's House

By William Seale

Published for the
Citizens Advisory Council for Interpreting
and Furnishing the Executive Mansion *by the*
Virginia State Library and Archives
Richmond • 1988

Standard Book Numbers: 0-88490-152-1 (case) 0-88490-153-x (paper)
©Virginia State Library and Archives 1988. All rights reserved.
Virginia State Library and Archives, Richmond, Virginia.
Printed in the United States of America.

To
Gay Montague Moore
1891–1988

CONTENTS

FOREWORD

WHEN the Citizens Advisory Council for Interpreting and Furnishing the Executive Mansion considered appropriate ways to commemorate the one-hundred-seventy-fifth anniversary of the mansion, the members felt that there should be popular events for citizens of all ages, restoration of the building itself, and scholarly studies. Thousands of visitors came to the mansion for special tours and for a one-hundred-seventy-fifth birthday party. The Advisory Council, in cooperation with the Department of General Services, commissioned measured drawings of the mansion by the Historic American Buildings Survey of the United States Department of the Interior. Architectural research, undertaken by the Historic Richmond Foundation and the Virginia Division of Historic Landmarks, determined the original appearance of the building and was the basis for its restoration in 1989. Last, but certainly not least, the council commissioned the writing of this book.

The mansion has been the subject of several other studies but none that presented its general history in a scholarly yet popular format. It was the council's goal to make available to the public in one volume both an account of the physical history of the house and the stories of some of its more interesting occupants and events. We feel William Seale has accomplished this for the enjoyment and edification of generations to come.

Without the enthusiastic support of the members of the Advisory Council, who voted to undertake this work, it would never have been published. We are particularly indebted to Helen R. Halpin, Mrs. Peter O. Ward, Jr., and Mrs. Harry L. Nash, whose enthusiasm for the mansion's projects inspires us all. We are also grateful for a generous gift from Paul Mellon.

Agreement by the Virginia State Library and Archives to publish the book assured that the proposal would become a reality. We are grateful for the interest of the State Librarian, Ella Gaines Yates, and many members of her staff, especially Jon Kukla and Emily Salmon. Sarah Shields Driggs, who did research first for Historic Richmond Foundation, then for William Seale, and finally for the State Library, has contributed significantly to all aspects of the project. Special thanks are also due to Dr. William H.

Higgins, Jr., Mary Jane Tayloe, Amanda T. Macaulay, and the trustees of the Historic Richmond Foundation.

We hope that this book will serve as a foundation for the ongoing study of the mansion and its occupants. It has been a pleasure and a privilege for the two of us to be involved in such an exciting and rewarding project. We know that past, present, and future members of the Citizens Advisory Council, as well as occupants of the mansion, will share our enthusiasm.

JEANNIE P. BALILES
JOHN G. ZEHMER, JR.

ACKNOWLEDGMENTS

P EOPLE who write history books, being always in pursuit of information, ask a lot of favors. I hope the book itself, finished and in print, thanks the many librarians, historians, and other specialists who helped me. Governor and Mrs. Gerald L. Baliles will find much to interest them here. They hold the mansion's history in high regard, and as we go to press are well into the restoration of the panels and balustrades to the facade of the house. John G. Zehmer, Jr., chairman of the Citizens Advisory Council on the mansion, is an architectural historian, and has shared with me his own research on the mansion's earliest configurations. I was fortunate to have the assistance of two gifted researchers during 1986 and 1987, Sarah Shields Driggs in Richmond, and Susan E. Smead in Charlottesville. They are familiar with the libraries and archives of the state, and mined their rich resources for the mansion's history. Sarah Shields Driggs subsequently amassed the illustrations for the book. Connie H. Wyrick's pioneering research reports on the mansion, begun during Governor Holton's administration, are excellent sources on historic furnishings and decorative arts. Any study of the house itself must begin with these.

Historian Jon Kukla coordinated publication of this book for the Virginia State Library and Archives. At the governor's house, Amanda T. Macaulay, Mrs. Baliles's executive assistant was always helpful, and Mary Jane Tayloe, mansion director, let me inspect the far corners of the house to help with my descriptions. Carl A. Ruthstrom assisted me in the preparation of the manuscript and its revisions and I thank him for his enthusiastic perseverance. T. Michael Miller of the Lloyd House Virginia Collection, Alexandria Library, and John H. Rhodehamel of the Huntington Library gave special assistance beyond what I had any right to expect. Others helped in other ways: Gary T. Scott, Sharon R. Saye, John P. Ridley, Rod Whealan, James B. Renberg, Denys Peter Myers, James M. Goode, Betty Monkman, Graham Hood, Lucia Stanton, and Yanek Brodski.

Last I thank three most particular residents of the commonwealth, Lucinda Smith Seale, William Seale III, and John Henry Broocks Seale, who live with me in Alexandria, only a few blocks from the old bank building where Civil War era Governor Pierpont ruled his Restored Virginia government, awaiting the day when he would go in triumph to the governor's mansion.

PREFACE

INSIDE the cast-iron fence of Capitol Square, the history of the commonwealth of Virginia is commemorated in the Capitol and the Executive Mansion. These two buildings have known nearly uninterrupted use since the early days of the state, and their story is intertwined with the public and private lives of those who have guided the political fortunes of Virginia. The story continues.

Thomas Jefferson searched the architectural past of the western world to find an appropriate model for the Capitol, and he selected a Roman temple. In architecture he thus drew a parallel between American statehood and the ancient republics. While the finishing touches were being added to the Virginia Capitol in 1798, Massachusetts was completing Boston's Georgian statehouse, a different idea entirely in state government architecture. Its designer, Charles Bulfinch, also based his plan on a foreign model but a modern one, Somerset House, a new government building in London.

The legislative houses at Richmond and Boston represented not only different architecture, but different notions of government. Jefferson's temple always seemed right for an independent-minded Virginia. Bulfinch's design cast a long shadow that rather quickly extended to Capitol Square. When in 1811 the commonwealth built the present Executive Mansion, it turned away from Jefferson's temple theme to a New England architect who designed the house in the Bulfinch manner.

The Capitol's history is woven into law books and written proceedings of the General Assembly. That of the mansion was not as fully recorded, yet the story of its architecture and furnishing and chain of occupants, presents more readily a chronicle of Virginia's past than the more complex Capitol story. The mansion's history is personal as well as architectural. Governors actually lived in the mansion, and still do, sharing public lives on Capitol Square with their families.

Governors and their wives sometimes kept diaries, or they or their kin might write memoirs. Where collections of their personal letters exist, they shed light on private life. Public places are subject to public scrutiny, so their records were kept then as now. For the mansion we have fairly complete household accounts, invoices, contracts, and documents of many kinds. Some administrations made meticulous inventories of the contents of the rooms.

It is the oldest continually occupied governor's mansion built for the purpose in the United States. The first occupant had moved in by March 12, 1813. For the thirty-seven years before that the commonwealth's governors endured discomfort and the General Assembly poured money into temporary houses. The mansion was designed to meet the needs of the office, which have changed, and the mansion has been altered to fit—but surprisingly little. While it seemed an expensive house when completed in 1813, it has proved to be one of the best investments the commonwealth of Virginia has ever made.

This book is a social history of the Executive Mansion from its building to the present time, neither architectural history in the strict sense, nor political history, nor a collection of governors' biographies. I have featured the house in the context of the larger human story, emphasizing the occupants and the alterations they carried out, particularly in the first one hundred twenty-five years, when the building achieved more or less its present form. Quite naturally some characters' lives are more closely tied to the mansion than others, either through the changes they made, or their zest for using it. These people claim the most space in the pages that follow.

Books about houses should be in part visual, with illustrations that amplify the narrative. For the early days of the mansion the images are scarce. Photography was not introduced until twenty-six years after the first governor moved in, and the drawings and paintings are few. Recent history has produced photographs in abundance. We cherish the nineteenth-century photographs for their information, but from the modern ones select the best from many possibilities. Where photographs or drawings of some kind do not exist, and I wish they did, I have substituted written descriptions as full as the documentation allows.

Alexandria, Virginia   WILLIAM SEALE

Virginia's Executive Mansion

Designed and built early in the eighteenth century, the Governor's Palace was one of the colony's most fashionable buildings. The only surviving image of the original building, which burned while being used as a hospital in 1781, is the detail in this large engraving, the Bodleian Plate, which also pictured Williamsburg's other official buildings.

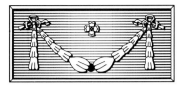

ONE

First Houses

A S the colony of Virginia provided an official residence for the royal governor, so the state, from the beginning, had a governor's house. Patrick Henry, first governor of the commonwealth, occupied the colonial Governor's Palace in Williamsburg, the same structure reconstructed there today. In scarlet cloak, black knee breeches, silver shoe buckles and powdered wig, the eloquent common-man exponent of American liberty took his oath of office on July 6, 1776, well before the good news of independence could have come by sail or hoof from Philadelphia.

Henry was a widower. His enormous household of relatives, children, and slaves—ultimately a total of some eighty people—filled the large old-fashioned brick pile that loomed tall and austere at the north end of Palace Green. Some of the English furnishings of the colonial governors remained for Henry to use—large mahogany pieces, some gilded mirrors, and the like—and the state appropriated £1,000 for repairs. The governor's children, "as wild as young colts," were his dearest friends and constant companions and "permitted to run quite at large" through the great halls and attics, the outbuildings and the park. Otherwise Henry ran the palace with the strict decorum that befitted his position.

A year after taking office Governor Patrick Henry married the youthful and wellborn Dorothea ("Dolly") Dandridge, of Hanover County. Their October wedding was followed in August by the birth of their first child at the palace. She was named Dorothea Spotswood Henry after her mother and a famous ancestor, Alexander Spotswood, the first British governor to occupy the palace. The Henrys departed Williamsburg on June 1, 1779, leaving the palace to Thomas Jefferson, the man chosen by the General Assembly as his successor.

Many years later Jefferson wrote frankly that the public might have had "more confidence in a military chief." It was wartime, and the British were carrying their offensive to the southern states. Jefferson inherited most of Henry's problems, while the War for Independence raged ever closer. The governor dared not risk his family's safety in a place so near the coast and vulnerable to attack by British vessels plying the Atlantic. A servant later recalled that Martha Jefferson and the two daughters spent some time with the governor at Williamsburg, but more often were hidden away with relatives on inland plantations. In idle moments the governor sketched plans for remodeling the palace, moving partitions, adding columns to the facade. On the inventory left by the sometimes careless Patrick Henry, Jefferson wrote clarifications and corrections.

In response to age-old political pressures and the immediate dangers of war, the capital was moved from Williamsburg to Richmond in the spring of 1780. Jefferson rented a house from his uncle, Thomas Turpin, near what is today the corner of Broad and Governor streets. This wooden town house stood on a sharp incline, not far from Capitol Square. Furnishings came overland from Williamsburg, and the Jeffersons were scarcely settled before

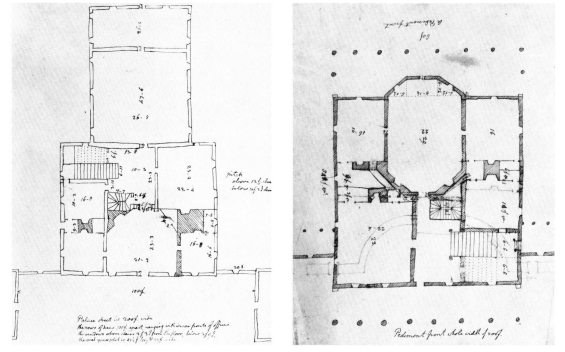

Coolidge Collection, Massachusetts Historical Society

Thomas Jefferson's measured drawing of the Governor's Palace (left) *shows the building as it probably stood when he lived there in 1780. In his* Notes on the State of Virginia, *Jefferson scathingly criticized Virginia's architecture, but commented that the palace was "capable of being made an elegant seat." Jefferson's ideas for remodeling the palace, sketched about the same time* (right), *reflected the latest architectural thought. His changes—two pedimented porches and a small projection to create an elongated octagonal room—would have resulted in a rectangular neoclassical temple-form building similar to the Virginia State Capitol, begun in 1785.*

4

a brief controversy erupted over his use of "Palace furniture" that some thought the state might sell to raise money to fight the war. Only a political tempest, it soon died down.

Thomas and Martha Jefferson's happy days in the rented "Palace" in Richmond were the only period in his public life that we see them together, host and hostess, at the principal scenes of activity. She was small and pretty, with large hazel eyes and auburn hair. Jefferson was a homebody, in contrast to the more gregarious Henry. He held a ball after the removal to Richmond, but more often the Jeffersons entertained small groups for dinner at home. Most of his days were spent meeting with the powerful Council of State in its nearby headquarters. The General Assembly met in a rented frame building at Fourteenth and Cary streets, a short walk downhill from the governor's house.

The administration was not peaceful and quiet. From the Turpin house on January 4, 1781, Jefferson evacuated the state government to escape capture by an invading army riding hard under Benedict Arnold. For this, accusations of personal cowardice were to be hurled at Jefferson by his fellow Virginians throughout the rest of his life.

Back in Richmond that spring tragedy struck the Jeffersons with the death of their infant daughter, Lucy. The British attacked again, and two weeks later the city was rescued by General Lafayette. This time Jefferson stayed put, but when British invaders returned yet a third time he was again forced to escape the city. One of his last acts in the rented governor's house was to receive a party of Illinois Indians and smoke the peace pipe with Brother John Baptist de Coigne and the tribal delegation.

Exactly when the second state-owned governor's house was built is uncertain. The house was there when the state acquired the land from James Marsden. Certainly it was old enough to have become run-down, but records of its construction are lost. It stood about where the present mansion stands, a wooden building with one or two brick ends containing chimneys. Old repair bills suggest that there were four rooms, and mention a porch. The earliest of these documents about the house, an order to the state's quartermaster to repair it and its outbuildings, is dated December 3, 1781.

The Marquis François Jean de Chastellux visited Governor Benjamin Harrison there on April 26, 1782: "I found him settled in a very plain, but spacious enough house, which had just been fitted up for him." The governor, a signer of the Declaration of Independence, was a giant, six feet four inches tall and weighing about two hundred fifty pounds. John Adams found him an "indolent, luxurious, heavy gentleman," but Chastellux enjoyed a delightful conversation, "unrestrained and agreeable, which he was even desirous of prolonging." Remembering the official surround-

American artist John Trumbull executed this miniature oil portrait of Thomas Jefferson during their months together in Paris during the winter of 1787-1788, while Jefferson was minister to France.

Anne Hill Carter Lee, mother of Robert E. Lee, married Governor Henry ("Light-Horse Harry") Lee and lived in the house that the mansion replaced.

View of the Capitol, Richmond, from Dr James Maceburg's Diningroom

June 1st 1797

In 1797 architect Benjamin Henry Latrobe sketched the Capitol in watercolor from the foot of Capitol Square. Along with the barren expanse of hillside and a guardhouse on the site of the present Bell Tower, Latrobe recorded a distant glimpse of the house that Governor John Tyler pronounced "intolerable for a private family" and that Richmond historian Samuel Mordecai described as "for many years unconscious of paint." From the architectural details visible in this tiny vignette, the entrance porch of the house apparently faced east toward present-day Governor Street.

ings, the marquis wrote, "there was nothing to distinguish him from other citizens."

This second governor's residence was available to twelve governors, although not all of them lived in it. The state constantly spent money for whitewashing, patching windows, shifting rooms in the basement, and adding outbuildings. Fences were put up and improved to thwart the goats and cattle that grazed Capitol Square. At least a few pieces of the furniture may have survived from the palace at Williamsburg but, to be sure, not many. Governor Harrison scouted around after the Revolution to retrieve furnishings scattered from the house and found only an old bed "of little value being worn out by militia & recovered from some low creature in the town." Mirrors, a sideboard with marble slab, and a tea table are mentioned in the records, but Governor James Wood wrote at the bottom of his inventory in 1796 that nearly everything was "ruined," and that the chairs, of which there were many, were "old and many of them broken."

Capitol Square in the late-eighteenth century was a grassy meadow, improved in the single circumstance that its native trees had been cut down. Several streets still ran through the unfenced square. Construction of the new Capitol had begun in the spring of 1785, and the area was littered with lumber sheds, stacks of bricks and other materials, and construction yards for the various tradesmen. A long gulley separated the governor's house from the remainder of the square. Deep, weed-grown, and subject to flooding, this hazardous ditch was crossed by means of a footbridge, which often washed away, or in dry weather simply by climbing down one side and up the opposite bank. A roadway was built across the narrowest part of the gulley, but most people probably approached the house from the east, where Governor Street passes behind the site to form the eastern boundary of Capitol Square.

Patrick Henry returned to the governorship in 1784, bringing his family to the wooden residence. From her windows Dolly Henry could see along the southwestern edge of the square, the soldiers' housing, with their chicken yards and their clotheslines filled with fluttering laundry. She made her calls in a fine coach provided to the governor by the state. At races or militia reviews the Henrys made a memorable couple, she young and pretty, the govenor carefully dressed always, and wearing a powdered wig. On May 1, 1785, the people of Richmond gathered in large number before the governor's house as the state's two most popular men sat down to dinner inside, Governor Henry and his guest George Washington.

Edmund Randolph, who followed Henry in office, left no records of his life in the house. He was probably seldom there; his own home was just a block to the west. Assigning his gubernatorial duties to the senior member of the Council, he was elected to the Virginia delegation to the Convention of 1787 at Philadelphia and served there during his term as governor. He proposed the Virginia Plan, and, while he declined to sign the Constitution when the convention adjourned, by June 1788 he was one of James Madison's allies at the Virginia Convention of 1788, where he supported ratification of the Constitution against Patrick Henry and other opponents. The elegant and learned Edmund Randolph was followed in office by Beverley Randolph, who had presided as lieutenant governor during his cousin's absence, and took a hardworking and creative approach when he shouldered the office in his own right. He ceded to the federal government the land—including the town of Alexandria—that became part of the District of Columbia until 1846. No records survive about his life in the official house.

The house was quiet during the Randolph years, but eventually it brightened again under Henry ("Light-Horse Harry") Lee, who took the oath of office on December 1, 1791. At first Lee was unhappy. His wife had died in childbirth during the year before his election, and the governor was in mourning. The house seemed closed up at first, with only business meetings and occasional small dinners. Lee was not happy. He tried to obtain a military command, and exchange grief and drudgery for adventure and glory, but it was not to be. In 1792 his eight-year-old son, Philip, died suddenly while the governor was absent. Servants buried the child in the yard of the governor's mansion, and confronted Lee with the sad news and the grave upon his return. The distraught governor ordered his boy exhumed for reburial beside his mother in the family tomb at Stratford Hall, the Lee family estate in Westmoreland County.

The widower soon married Anne Hill Carter, of Shirley plantation, in June 1793, the groom thirty-seven and the bride twenty. The governor's house came alive with entertaining, and parties of friends journeyed with him by boat downriver to Shirley. George Washington, observing the change in tempo, congratulated his revolutionary war comrade on having "exchanged the rugged and dangerous field of Mars for the soft and pleasurable bed of Venus."

Among the celebrities who called on the newlyweds at the residence was Citizen Edmond Genêt, the representative of the French republic, who hoped to lure the United States to the side of France in the war with England. Better to serve his accelerated social life, Governor Lee ordered an expansion of the kitchen with the purchase of an iron stove, boilers, cake molds, and various other culinary devices. Lee maintained a fine coach-and-four at his own expense, and eight slaves served in his house. As was his custom, Light-Horse Harry Lee spent his own money recklessly, but he was stingy when it came to spending public money on the house. He made necessary repairs to the foundation and saved the chimneys from toppling. Still, his expenditures of state funds were small compared to those of his successors James Wood, who added "china work," or Anglo-Chinese fretwork, to the stair railings, and James Monroe, who in his first of two terms remodeled the house inside and out and bought an assortment of items ranging from fine drawing-room furniture to "a Large Chicken Coop . . . with two Apartments."

Monroe's beautiful wife, Elizabeth, of New York, was the daughter of a West Indian merchant ruined by the Revolution. Both the governor and his lady were conscious of style, with a decided preference for things French; in the intimacy of the family circle they and their children always addressed each other in French. The handsome furniture they had purchased in Paris while he was American minister to France may have adorned the mansion. They later used it at the White House, and it is preserved today by the James Monroe Law Office–Museum in Fredericksburg. Their country home in Albemarle County, Highlands (now called Ash Lawn), was a simple place, but they planned a grander house someday. On his annual salary of $3,333 the governor was not rich. Still he required a setting suitable to his plans for elegant living, and at first refused to move his family into the mansion, renting a house until the necessary repairs were completed. The house was ready by late August 1800.

That same month Governor Monroe learned of a conspiracy led by the slave Gabriel and his brothers Solomon and Martin to attack Richmond and spark a massive slave revolt. Terror soon spread throughout Virginia as whites recalled the carnage of the 1791 slave rebellion in Santo Domingo. Bad weather on August 30, 1800, disrupted the conspirators' plans, and a vigilant militia acting on the word of several informers arrested dozens of slaves in Henrico and Caroline counties. Gabriel was captured in September trying to escape by boat through Norfolk. He was brought in chains, mounted on a horse, before the governor in front of the governor's house. Tall, handsome, and proud, Gabriel astonished onlookers with his majesty in the face of defeat and, inevitably, of death. Monroe talked with him in his cell at the penitentiary, hoping that before he was hanged he would tell what he knew, but the governor found that Gabriel had "made up his mind to die" and "resolved to say but little on the subject of the conspiracy."

Governor Monroe's tenure was tarnished by sorrow over the death of his only son, an infant, while he lived in the residence. This left an emotional wound from which neither Monroe nor his wife ever really recovered, but they withdrew into themselves and from then on made a sharp distinction between their public and private lives. In politics a high point in Monroe's governorship was the election of Jefferson to the presidency. An ardent Republican, the governor was both a friend and an admirer of Jefferson. He called for state funds to illuminate the newly completed Capitol and other public buildings of Richmond on March 4, 1801, the night of Jefferson's inauguration. The city shimmered with candlelight, and a magnificent dinner was held in the Capitol. Governor Monroe toasted the Union.

John Tyler, Sr., and his family lived in the state's dilapidated house on the site of the mansion. His son John read law in Richmond during his father's administration, later served as governor himself, and was the tenth president of the United States.

If the second residence had any admirers during its last years they did not set down their feelings on paper. The building proved too small, too shabby, and too poorly constructed to be reinforced. Furnishings wore out, disappeared, and were replaced by new tables, chairs, and wardrobes. Wallpaper decorated some of the rooms. A youthful John Tyler, son of Governor John Tyler and later president, remembered a landscape "untamed and unbroken." Capitol Square was barren and, he thought, probably not even fenced. "The Governor's house, at that time called the palace, was a building that neither aspired to architectural taste in its construction or consulted the comfort of its occupants in its interior arrangements."

The younger Tyler was put in charge of the grand dinner held by his father in honor of Jefferson's retirement from the presidency. It was October 1809 and Jefferson was in Richmond on business. Although home to the Democratic-Republican group known as the Richmond Junto, the capital itself was a Federalist bastion antagonistic to Jefferson's Democratic-Republican politics. Governor Tyler, a great admirer of the former president, intended to play the role of healer. John Tyler, Jr., dressed the waiters in matching livery and saw that every detail of the dinner was magnificently carried out. At the climax of the event, the waiters marched in with not one but two large plum puddings, ablaze.

"Two plum-puddings, John?" exclaimed the father, *"Two* plum-puddings? Why, this is rather extraordinary!"

"Yes sir," replied the son, rising and bowing to the guest of honor, "but it is an *extraordinary occasion!"*

Governor Tyler appeared before the legislature late in his administration and in the course of a long address said that the governor's house "is intolerable for a private family, there being not a foot of ground that is not exposed to three streets, besides a cluster of dirty tenements immediately in front of the house with their windows opening into the enclosure." This was followed on February 13, 1811, by an act of the General Assembly that authorized the new mansion and the rental of a better house in Richmond for the governor until the new house was ready.

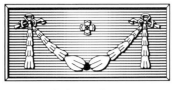

TWO

The Mansion Is Built

PLANS for the governor's mansion were drawn in the spring of 1811 and the house was officially occupied two years later, in March 1813. Where public works are often storm-tossed by controversy, this project seems to have gone smoothly and quickly.

Two weeks after authorizing the new house, the General Assembly appropriated $12,000 to build it "on the lot on which the present governor's house stands." A building committee composed of seven citizens rented a house at Ninth and Marshall streets for the governor and invited bids for the removal of the old "palace." Meanwhile, Governor James Monroe, serving his second term, resigned his office in April 1811 to join President James Madison's cabinet as secretary of state. When he left early, the committee filled the rented house with as much of the state's furnishings as it would hold and stored the remainder in one of the old wooden outbuildings at the construction site.

George William Smith commenced his official duties as acting governor on April 3, 1811, and probably remained in his own home in Shockoe Valley rather than moving to the tenement house. Bidding for the old residence brought $530 from Charles Copeland, but Copeland did not hurry to vacate the public lot. When he finally removed the building, he seems to have left the chimneys, their bricks to be salvaged later. The committee appointed from among its own number the carpenter William McKim as superintendent of the project, and selected as "undertaker," or contractor, Christopher Tompkins, another prominent figure in the Richmond building trades. For plans, the committee turned to Alexander Parris, who had come to Richmond to build a house for the local businessman John Bell.

Parris was in his thirties, a native of Massachusetts reared in Maine. As a young man he had made the change from carpenter to housewright to architect, and possessed remarkable gifts in his field. His early achievements are associated with Portland, Maine, where he started out, and in middle age with Boston, where he achieved fame. Richmond, his home for only two years, fell in between. Had Alexander Parris never left Portland, his

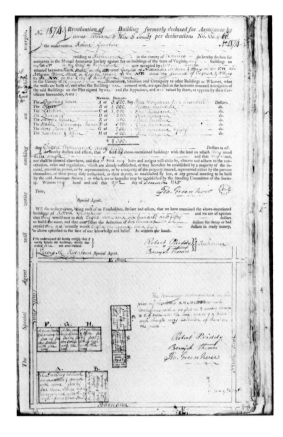

In a March 1813 announcement about her new boarding school for young ladies, Mrs. Broome identified her house as having been recently vacated by Governor James Barbour. An 1815 insurance policy (left) *described this brick house—one of several in which the governors lived before the mansion was built—on Bank Street at the foot of Capitol Square. Alexander Parris* (right) *designed the new Executive Mansion.*

importance in American architecture would likely have been less. As it happened, his travels and observation of the American architectural scene broadened his taste beyond the lessons offered by the architectural pattern books he had studied in his youth. Parris was exposed to some of the finest and most original building then taking place in the United States, and he had an enormous appetite for his craft. Journeying south from Maine, he observed the work of accomplished practitioners in his field, the English-born Benjamin Henry Latrobe in Philadelphia and Richmond, and Robert Mills in Philadelphia, himself a former pupil of Latrobe. In their work he found a more archaeological style than he had known in New England and also the Greek Revival, in which Parris would play a leading role.

When Alexander Parris appeared in Richmond he was still spellbound by the work of Boston's premier architect Charles Bulfinch, with whom he collaborated in later years. Bulfinch's highly personal adaptation of eighteenth-century Adamesque neoclassicism to the smaller scale of

American buildings and to red brick and wood instead of stone left its mark on New England for several generations. Alexander Parris was only one of many architects strongly influenced by this master, and it was the Bulfinch style that inspired the governor's mansion.

Building trades are always among the first struck by economic adversity, and so it was in New England early in the nineteenth century, when dangers at sea and commercial embargoes during the Napoleonic Wars slowed wheels of progress that had spun rapidly since the Revolution. For the time, undimmed prosperity in the South attracted men out of work. The exact circumstances of Alexander Parris's relocation in booming Richmond are not known, except that he carried with him a contract to build the house for John Bell. Within a year he found a second client, John Wickham, for whom he built the elegant neoclassical house in stucco that today forms part of the Valentine Museum. His transition to the new archaeological style is first seen in this fine urban dwelling.

The second decade of the new century was an especially lively period of building in Richmond. The city was a crossroads for the building trades. So fine a building as the Monumental Church, for example, required stone carvers and masons. Wickham needed skilled joiners to build the dramatic bowed room and circular stair inside his house. Daniel Raynerd moved from Boston to Richmond to practice his trade of ornamental plastering, embellishing interiors with handsome moldings and cast-plaster leaves, flowers, and classical figures. The Englishman George Bridport, decorative painter, had known great success in New York and Philadelphia. For Dolley Madison he adorned the ceiling of the Blue Room. Soon enough, big jobs attracted this celebrated "decorator" to Richmond. Alexander Parris was not

Virginia Museum of Fine Arts, gift of
John Barton Payne
Chester Harding's portrait of
Governor James Barbour, the
mansion's first resident, hangs
today in the Executive Mansion.

I am authorised to sell for cash or on a short credit the materials which the old palace, (or governor's house) is composed, the framing is extraordinary good—For terms apply to the Subscriber, who wishes to employ 4 or 5 good Carpenters or Joiners, to whom constant employment and generous wages will be given : none need apply but those that are steady and industrious.

C. TOMPKINS,

July 19. 3t

Virginia State Library and Archives
Old newspaper advertisements chronicled the disposal of the dilapidated early governor's house and progress toward the construction of the Executive Mansion. Christopher Tompkins, the contractor, was also a leader in the militia, shipbuilder, and ship captain.

alone nor necessarily the most important of the immigrants working in the Richmond building community.

As he was already in the employ of two rich and prominent citizens, Parris seemed an obvious choice to a state committee seeking a design for the governor's mansion. The committee paid him fifty dollars for his drawings, not an especially low figure for house plans at the time. All that now survives of his original design is a sketch in his notebook of the main floor. This drawing shows the basic floor plan as built, with some modifications such as altered locations for fireplaces and windows. No other drawings have been found. Architects did not normally make the extensive working drawings that are customary today; Parris may have supplied only three or four sheets. The usual procedure was for the architect to supply the plan of rooms and elevations of the various facades, drafting only as many details of woodwork, windows, doors, and staircases as he was asked to provide or as he needed to convey his design. Details of construction were devised by the contractor and various specialized tradesmen.

Parris's floor plan indicates that he designed the house more or less as we know it, except for the porches and additions to the rear. Aware that the previous residence had been too small, the committee probably suggested the size of the building. Although even larger today, the mansion was a big house from the start, with broad halls and ample rooms for living and entertaining, all somewhat superior in scale even to large Virginia houses of

16

the time. The sharply inclined lot allowed for a full basement at ground level on two sides with two full stories above. Only the two upper floors were visible from Capitol Square. Storage and service rooms were planned for the basement, with the formal entrance and parlors on the middle or first floor and bedchambers for the governor's family upstairs.

The new house did not rise from precisely the same site as the old, for construction was underway by July 1811, and the old house was not demolished until 1812. Smith took a strong interest in the mansion, buying various furnishings to use himself until the house was ready. On his orders the state purchased a Gothic secretary, Windsor chairs, and tableware. Of the construction site we know nothing. Had the documents survived, invoices would doubtless identify the suppliers of brick, the names of the brickmasons and their apprentices, and perhaps the laborers whose hoes, shovels, and rakes graded the steep slope around the house. Politicians, including the governor, liked to stop by and inspect all state building projects. They were ready with suggestions, for men naturally aspire to build.

In certain respects, all building projects proceed about the same. In the fall, when the air becomes too cold for setting mortar, work stops and the site is wintered in. By November 1811 cold winds were whipping Capitol Square. The brickmasons stopped, packing the newest of the brick walls in dirt and straw for protection against freezing. The carpenters' hall, on the other hand, was warmed by stoves and remained in operation year-round. Some workmen were living there in December when the governor met a terrible death by fire in the great disaster at the Richmond Theater. On the day after Christmas during a lamplit pantomime the scenery caught fire on stage, and the house itself was soon blazing. More than seventy people died, including George William Smith. His remains, along with those of most of the other casualties, were buried in a vault beneath the Monumental Church erected in their memory a few hundred yards northeast of the mansion.

Smith's interest in the mansion was shared and perhaps even exceeded by Governor James Barbour. He came to office on January 4, 1812, after the week-long acting governorship of Peyton Randolph, senior member of the Council of State and the third man to occupy the office in that single term. Barbour liked houses. His own neoclassical mansion, Barboursville, in Orange County, was designed by his friend and neighbor Thomas Jefferson and finished in the decade after Barbour's term as governor, and, today a burnt-out ruin, it still rises in columned magnificence over thick plantings of boxwood and mown lawns.

Governor Barbour's plantation lands were vast, his slaves many, and his tastes throughout his life exacting and expensive. An ardent Republican, he was a good businessman and experimental farmer, with the leisure to enter politics. A handsome and memorable man, he had a touch of the martinet

in his manner but it seldom overshadowed his stronger qualities. As governor, Barbour exuded optimism, even when faced with the grim prospect of the war with England.

Barbour moved with his wife into a rented governor's house at Christmas 1812 after living for nearly a year by himself in a hotel. He watched the walls rise for the governor's house, and saw its roof shingled. Several major changes in the original plan were made after Barbour took office, for which in February 1812 the General Assembly appropriated an additional $8,000. The changes included adding two side porches and replacing under fewer roofs the haphazard clutter of old wooden outbuildings. Paramount among the new structures was the two-story brick servants' quarters and kitchen that still stands today, tucked against the south slope and well apart from the mansion itself, out of view, for the most part, from the square itself.

The new icehouse was mounted over a cool, brick-lined pit dug deep into the ground and equipped with drains. Layers of ice were packed tightly in sawdust or straw, slowing the melting process to such an extent that the governor could enjoy ice year-round. A stable was not part of the original plan, but Barbour ordered a new one built in 1813. Of frame construction, it had rolling doors to the outside and some brick flooring within. The carriage yard probably was paved with bricks from the earlier house. Somewhere nearby stood a wooden washhouse, with its caldrons, fire grates, ironing boards, and clotheslines inside and out.

The committee may have simplified Parris's ideas for the interior and then, during construction, had to yield to elaborations urged by Governor Barbour. For the entrance hall, Parris could have intended groin vaulting simulated in plaster over wooden lath. The notebook plan suggests the necessary column supports for such a design. While this detail may never have been submitted, it would not be surprising to find it here as in other interiors designed by Parris in the Bulfinch vein. Inspiration for the plaster cornice that survives in the hall today, richly detailed in vines, leaves, and neoclassical motifs, came from William Pain's *The Practical House Carpenter,* a popular architectural design book published in its fifth London edition in 1794 and its first American edition in Boston two years later. This sourcebook was certainly known to Parris, but it was just as readily available to William McKim, Christopher Tompkins, or Governor Barbour himself, for the many editions of Pain's books were widely used in late-eighteenth- and early-nineteenth-century Virginia.

Extensive grading was undertaken around the house, as soon as the outside brick walls were completed. A significant effort was made to fill the gully that divided the mansion lot from the rest of the square, a ravine that had kept the square looking more like a pasture than the intended reflection of a Roman forum. This measure was not entirely successful, however, for the water would reclaim some of its old path in hard rains. Still the grading

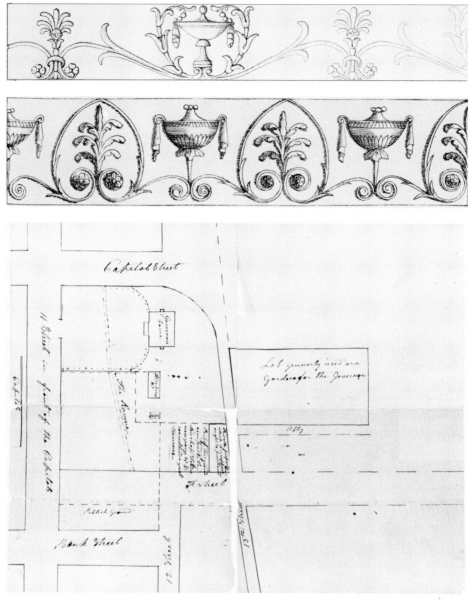

Measured drawings by the Historic American Buildings Survey (top)
*document the mansion as it stood in 1987. This detail of ornament from the
entrance hall* (middle) *shows the delicate plasterwork of torches, draped
urns, and foliage inspired by a popular architectural pattern book of the
period, William Pain's* Practical House Carpenter. *The commissioners
hired two carpenters to measure all aspects of the completed house and
recommend appropriate compensation for Tompkins. Several changes in
the plans had been made, including the addition of the small side porches
that can be seen on the commissioners' plat* (bottom). *For these changes,
Tompkins was paid almost three thousand dollars more than the originally
contracted price.*

of 1812 and 1813, piecemeal though it seems to have been, was the beginning of a unified Capitol Square.

About a month before Governor Barbour moved in, the commissioners submitted their final report to the General Assembly. Wise politicians, they were careful to cover themselves in describing a bit more of a house than the legislators had set out to build. Mindful of "the honor and dignity of the state" as well as the "conveniency of the Chief Magistrate," the commissioners had seen "the principal story of said building . . . finished off in a style rather superior to that originally contemplated" and erected "two plain porches on the north and south fronts of said building." Even so, they wished more could be done with the "exterior view of the building" and more for the "comfort and conveniency of its inhabitants." They recommended adding a parapet or "the superstructure of a terrace" above the eaves, building "a portico to the door fronting the Capitol," and improving the fireplaces with "marble hearths and slabs . . . substituted for the plain . . . brick ones."

The formal measurement of the mansion took place in January and February 1813. This age-old process—now long abandoned—was at that time a common means of determining payment for construction work. Client and builders agreed upon "two disinterested and competent characters" as referees, in this case the carpenters Alexander McKim for the commonwealth and Wilson Bryan for Tompkins. Holding final authority, the referees inspected the work in all particulars, measuring it and through the application of certain formulas determining the value of each craftsman's labor. The house itself, materials included, appraised at $14,525.53.

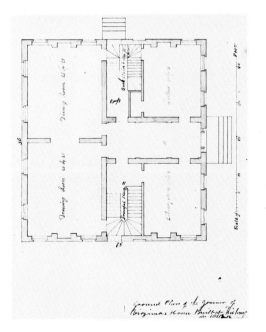

American Antiquarian Society, Worcester, Massachusetts
Original mansion plans by architect Alexander Parris have not survived. This later drawing, found in the architect's sketchbook, is the only surviving plan in Parris's hand. Modified during construction, the house does not have fireplaces on the outside walls and some other details shown in this drawing.

Kitchen, smokehouse, "necessary," fencing, and grading added another $3,986.29. Alexander McKim received $60 for his valuation as a referee, and his brother William McKim was paid $300 "for the superintendency, planning, &c. of the work." The grand total came to $18,871.82—leaving a balance of $1,128.18 from the appropriations "a part of which, will be necessarily consumed in finishing the enclosure."

A handsome house it was. Lofty and important looking, the rectangular facade was perched on the edge of the hill, but the level, graveled ground at the front gave a base visually, masking the drop of the ground to the rear. Nothing stood near enough to offer competition or obstruction to the mansion itself. The crisp, external skin of brick was laid in Flemish bond, a pattern favored for both its beauty and durability in Virginia's finest architecture and in the best brick buildings in America. Originally there was no front porch, as is there today, only wooden steps up to a door surmounted by a semicircular window or fanlight.

Stone windowsills delicately "tooth tooled" in vertical stripes and stuccoed flat arches, with prominent keystones, defined the principal windows. Rectangular stuccoed panels were recessed between the windows of the first and second floors, a device familar in New England houses of this sort, but here perhaps borrowed more directly from the Capitol as a means of relating the two buildings. An 1826 pencil sketch of the Capitol with the mansion in the background—the earliest depiction of the mansion—shows the panels unornamented, but from an early date these panels had plaster decorations representing garlands of flowers swagged from ribbon bows. A wood-shingled roof rose from the eaves to a lofty deck, defined at its corners by tall chimneys. In 1823 the commonwealth connected the four chimneys by means of wooden balustrades, which fenced the deck for safe use as an observatory and crowned the finished house.

At the time the mansion was first occupied in March 1813, America had been at war with England for nine months. The governor expected an attack on the Virginia coast at any moment. Anxious that his state be ready, he was often away from Richmond rallying the populace with dramatic speeches. While some of the more sophisticated listeners blushed occasionally at the Caesarean magnificence of the governor's orations, most people seem to have approved. Barbour got the reaction he wanted.

When he was at home in the mansion, life seems to have been less than private for James and Lucy Barbour and their three children. They started a tradition of hospitality in the new house. Besides the dinners and receptions for which they sent out written invitations, or "cards," any legislator was welcome to enter the state's house during the session and make himself at home.

The dining room, to the right at the end of the entrance hall, was kept supplied with food and drink. On the sideboard Governor Barbour's silver punch bowl brimmed with strong whiskey punch, cooled with ice from the icehouse. A thirsty legislator had only to dip the ladle and fill his cup. Servants kept watch to replenish the bowl. This particular mode of refreshment became a tradition in the governor's house until later nineteenth-century ideas of temperance inspired its abolition and a more private approach.

Hardly had the Barbours been in the mansion three weeks when the British began harrying the Virginia coast, and in midsummer their ships had advanced up the James as far as Williamsburg. News of these invasions caused general panic, but the British departed, not to come back for a year. When they landed at Norfolk in 1814, they were all the more feared as the invaders who had burned the national capital. Governor Barbour called out the militia. Richmond became an armed camp.

"Everywhere the calls was 'To Arms! To Arms!'" a citizen later recalled, "and every day the Capitol Square was made a parade ground." Standing

Massachusetts Historical Society, Boston
Virginia State Library and Archives

Charles Bulfinch's sketch for the first Harrison Gray Otis House (left) *illustrates Alexander Parris's early inspiration, the Adamesque buildings of Boston. The earliest-known image of the Executive Mansion facade, a faint 1826 pencil sketch* (right), *in the background of a drawing of the Capitol shows Parris's adaptation. The mansion door was soon altered by the addition of a neoclassical porch, and, in 1830, a parapet at the lower edge of the roof that balanced the balustrade connecting the chimneys.*

bareheaded before the mansion the governor reviewed the proud troops marching in formation, boasting weeks and months of drilling. Thousands passed by, summer and autumn. Local companies paraded the most regularly, the Richmond Light Infantry Blues, the Richmond Rifles, and the darlings of the city, the Junior Blues, boys under fifteen. Once again Richmond was spared.

Governor Barbour turned the mansion over to his successor, Wilson Cary Nicholas, on December 1, 1814, and retired to his home. That Christmas the war was at its low ebb, but the early days of 1815 brought the news of the Treaty of Ghent and more, Andrew Jackson's miraculous victory at New Orleans. Virginia and the nation sensed triumph profoundly.

Our knowledge of the appearance of the mansion's interior before the 1820s is vague. Only with that decade do inventories and other papers of the house appear in the archives in some abundance. Governor Barbour had bought furniture with state funds in 1811 and 1812. On January 27, 1813, the General Assembly appropriated $3,000 for furniture. Many original invoices for the actual purchases are lost, so descriptions are impossible.

Governor Nicholas seems to have shown very little interest in the house. He and his wife, Margaret Smith Nicholas, did live there, but he never acted as though it was home. Visitors remembered her more than him. She was the romantic sort, once the friend and ever the defender of Major John André, the engaging British spy hanged during the American Revolution. There are warm accounts of her delightful stories, her "fashionable style of dress." The governor stayed close to his work, a dignified gentleman who preferred to accept hospitality elsewhere in town than to extend his own. "The office I am in," he wrote, "suits me as little as I suit it."

Governor Nicholas did, however, take an interest in Capitol Square. Some plans had been drawn locally, but the governor rejected them. Encouraged perhaps by Margaret Nicholas, a member of a prominent Baltimore family, he commissioned the French émigré Maximilian Godefroy to plan the transformation of the square from pasture to park. The governor wanted not only an appropriate setting for the Capitol but also a park for promenading with views of the city's high elevations and the river's beautiful valley. A military engineer in his native France, Godefroy had immigrated in 1805, taught architecture and engineering in Baltimore, and designed Saint Mary's Chapel, the first Gothic Revival church in the United States, as well as Baltimore's Battle Monument.

When Godefroy arrived in July 1816 a room was set up for him in the Capitol, where he could work under the eye of the governor and keep his door open so the legislators might "examine the progress of his labors." The engineer seems to have agreed to this uncomfortable situation in the hope

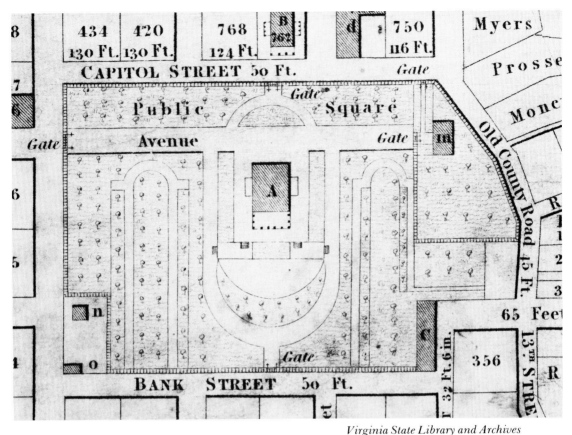

An 1835 map shows those parts of Godefroy's 1816 landscape plan for Capitol Square that were implemented and maintained. The crescent-shaped terracing and north-south walks flanked by trees, created parklike allées in a formal French style that Godefroy believed most appropriate to a seat of government.

that he could impress the politicians sufficiently to snare more state work. Godefroy's drawings are lost, but his plan survives in old maps and views of the city and later plans of Capitol Square. The landscape design was made in the French baroque manner, with orderly terraces, allées of trees, and semicircular promenades steplike in the hillside below the Capitol.

Implementation of the plan was in the hands of John P. Shields, the man who had been working at grading the square since 1812. His teams of workmen, occupied so long moving earth with wheelbarrows and carts, now turned to creating Godefroy's terraces. Six years later, having moved tons of dirt and planted hundreds of trees, Shields bemoaned the ambitious plan and the many changes that had reduced his own profits to losses. His farm was under mortgage, his workmen "barefoot and naked."

It may be that a broad double line of trees leading to the mansion was planted at this time. Godefroy's plan ran a straight avenue east from Ninth Street to the mansion (extending the line of modern Grace Street). Such a formal situation for the house demanded some embellishment. In Civil War

25

photographs taken some forty years after Godefroy's trees were planted, they appear in great number full-size, growing close together in straight lines. A few of Godefroy's trees may remain today, but the allée is gone. The graveled area immediately in front of the mansion was packed flat by stone rollers, making it more a wide terrace than a driveway, the surface wetted and compressed to serve man and horse with a minimum of mud and dust.

James Patton Preston, governor from 1816 to 1819, willingly pursued the work on the square. For the house he bought only odds and ends, fire screens, Brussels carpeting, a coffee pot, a substantial amount of china, and a dozen "fancy chairs." He left no comment as to how the governor's mansion looked inside in the early days. His successor, Thomas Mann Randolph, left us a little more information: orders from a local cabinet-maker, Robert Poore, for beds, tables, "pair claw card tables," and the like. He ordered the featherbeds, or mattresses, weighed, and as a result figures survive to indicate that Randolph's household slept comfortably.

Under Randolph the mansion's domestic scene was stormy. The governor had married Thomas Jefferson's daughter Martha, called Patsy, who was closely attached to her father. She had all the graces, and Randolph had few, or at least that was the interpretation everyone accepted, including the Randolphs' themselves. Under her father's instruction, Patsy Randolph had grown to love books, while her burly husband liked horses and the out-of-doors. Even his scholarly interest in botany seems not to have provided a common ground between them. Having run Monticello since girlhood, she was adept at domestic management, yet she stayed with her husband at the mansion as little as possible, passing her days instead at Edgehill, in Albemarle County, or with her father, who with the selfishness of old age often summoned her to his side.

Randolph was left alone most of the time, his tendency to depression turning him often to heavy drink. He once said that his manners had come from the "blunt school of agriculture," and that he cared little for "forms used for mere respect." Toward the end of his administration he began holding weekly political dinners, which his wife sometimes attended. Indeed Randolph's greatest support was from the western counties, and he filled his table in the mansion with their representatives. One of Mrs. Randolphs relatives described these guests as "savages from the west." His daughters denounced the "rowdies," and demanded "that the company be varied a little." The girls drew up a guest list for "a very genteel party," restricted only to the "cream of the legislature," but the altered tone was brief. Jefferson, insofar as it is known, never came to call.

Our first intimate glimpse of life inside the mansion comes with the administration of James Pleasants, governor from 1822 to 1825. The charming, mild-mannered Pleasants, from an old farming family of the Richmond area, was a veteran of about twenty-five years in politics when he became governor. In the mansion he and his wife, Susanna Rose, lived in quiet gentility. They made an inventory of the house after they moved in, and a second inventory was made two days after they left, listing the contents of the mansion room-by-room.

Public houses and their furnishings wear faster than private ones. The governor's house was only ten years old, but it had witnessed the beautiful entertainments of the Barbours and the raucous dinners of Thomas Mann Randolph. In spite of Governor Preston's new carpets, the interior of the house apparently needed work, and repair and decorating projects recurred throughout the 1820s. Governor Pleasants did many of them, and from his accumulated invoices together with his inventories and several later ones we can describe the interior as is existed about 1830.

The great fanlight doorway opened into a broad lofty entrance hall, divided dramatically by a sweeping arch and crowned with a neoclassical cornice. The hall seemed a confluence of doors. In so public a house, access was necessarily controlled, hence there were doors to everything. These shiny portals, grained with paint to imitate oak, gave entry into two rooms in front and two in the back. Beyond the great central arch, two doors stood side by side, forming an abruptly commonplace conclusion to the hall and opening into the dining room and drawing room. In 1824 the hall had been carpeted, and an old dining-room table had been placed against one wall with chairs for the governor's incessant business callers, those not welcomed beyond the dining-room door for a taste of punch.

In the nineteenth century, governors received nearly all their callers, and these sessions took place in the first room to the left as one entered at the front door. They were kept as brief as politeness would allow. The room was simply furnished, with a pine table, a big "old fashioned" mirror that may have come from the palace in Williamsburg, and a washstand in the corner. The monotony of books and papers was relieved only by one curiosity, the plaster model Thomas Jefferson had ordered in Paris forty years earlier to transmit with his design for the Virginia Capitol. This artifact seems to have stayed with the governors in the early days; later it was usually on display in the Capitol, where it can be seen today.

Across the hall from this office, the little parlor (as the southwest room came to be called over the years) was crowded with a sideboard, two sofas covered in stiff horsehair, and many straight chairs, painted green, varnished, and gilded. The little parlor was a tall room with tall windows, apparently not covered by curtains—a place for receiving brief social calls from politician's wives and citizens from Richmond, a place where dinner guests gathered upon arrival before being escorted deeper into the house.

Each of two skylighted staircases located in separate side corridors off the back corners of the hall served a different purpose. While today they seem a matching pair, originally they looked quite different. The better stair on the left was the formal means of ascent to the upper floor. The corresponding stair to the south was smaller and steeper for the use of servants. A narrow stairway descended beneath it to the basement and a ground-level outside door to the kitchen and servants' quarters.

The finest rooms in the house lay beyond the doors at the end of the hall, the dining room on the right and drawing room on the left. In their dimensions the two rooms although distinctly separate were the same size, together running the entire length of the back of the house. From the time the house was first occupied to the present, the main social events of the governors have taken place here. The two rooms were thrown into one in 1906 to make the present ballroom. Each originally had a fireplace, decorative cornice, wooden door and window trim, and broad-plank floors of unfinished pine that were always concealed by carpeting or straw matting. Passage between the rooms was by means of a double door in their common wall. In most respects the interiors seem to have matched architecturally, and in spite of their different functions they were furnished rather alike.

For the dining room the state had bought a long mahogany dining table in three parts, set up on brass casters. Eighteen cane-bottomed, red-painted chairs were pulled up to it, and it would have been typical for the wooden venetian blinds at the windows to have matched the chairs in color. The large accumulation of the state's china and glassware was kept in a mahogany sideboard and a big double-door china "press." Additional presses of walnut and pine also served for storage. An inventory of 1825 listed 489 pieces of china, glass, and silver plate in the dining room, including imported Chinese "canton," several "blue printed" pitchers, cut-glass decanters, 16 "waiters" or trays, 40 glass tumblers, and silver-plated bowls and candlesticks.

Food was served to this room from the two-story brick kitchen in the side yard, a whole story lower than the main floor of the house. There was no roof over the walkway that connected the kitchen to the main house, so the governor's meals were carried across an open dirt yard—perhaps on a brick walk—into the basement and up the service stairs to the dining room.

Keeping the food hot was a chore and a science. Meals were served in courses; all serving dishes had tops. Servants used a fireplace in the basement to heat the food en route from kitchen to table. Dinner plates were warmed in a tin warmer before the dining-room fireplace, and, while no cooking was done there, water for coffee and tea was boiled over coals raked out on the hearth. Finishing touches might be put on any number of dishes after the food reached the dining room, the butler performing his skills at the sideboard. After dinner the usable leftovers were kept in wire "safes" in the basement, rather than being returned to the kitchen outside.

The drawing-room furniture resembled that in the dining room. Twenty-one red-and-gilt rush-bottomed chairs stood along the walls with the pair of matching red-painted sofas, and two more sofas upholstered in horsehair. Over the mantel a mirror with a gilded frame reflected the room and diffused the light from the windows. It was a splendor that we today might have difficulty appreciating. In winter the chilly rooms smelled of the sooty fireplaces around which their numerous chairs were clustered. Springtime saw the raising of the tall windows of ripply glass to admit the perfumes of nearby pastures. For summer the rooms were made as barren as they could be. The visitors' general impression of these formal rooms was of large, plastered spaces that the fireplaces would not warm, of sprawling fields of wall-to-wall carpeting—both fine Brussels and the relatively cheap, thin ingrain in the same room—and of heavy curtains of wool moreen in perhaps fiery red, bright yellow, or cool green. For intimate family gatherings the rooms must have seemed too big, and for the press of New Year's callers, too small.

More comfort was found in the four bedrooms upstairs, where a mixture of new and old furnishings filled chambers not meant for the public eye. Some rooms had window curtains, some did not, but the beds were curtained against winter drafts. A mixture of fine featherbeds and the utilitarian corn-shuck mattresses provided comfort beyond that enjoyed by many private citizens. Central to the second floor, over the entrance hall, a locked storeroom housed extra furniture from all the other rooms and protected the valuables of the house. The best of the state table silver was kept there in trunks. Long after a dinner or ball was over, the governor's wife stood by the door counting with the butler the silver knives and forks and the plates and other china as they were brought up from the dining room, where they had been washed. A full accounting was required at the administration's close .

By the close of 1830 the mansion's exterior looked more or less as we see it today. Over the summer of that year a parapet was built along the edge of the roof—as the building committee had recommended in 1813—and "three porches and a front door" were built, two on the sides replacing the first ones and a new "portico" facing the square. To accommodate the front porch, the fan window over the door was cut down to a rectangular transom. The press was pleased. "By the addition of Porticoes and Colonnade," extolled the *Richmond Whig*, the governor's house had been transformed from "being externally, one of the homeliest dwellings in Richmond" to a stately appearance "now entitled to the appellation of elegance."

Between festive engagements on his Richmond visits during his 1824–1825 tour of the United States, the Marquis de Lafayette found time to sit for an enormous full-length portrait by Richmond painter Edward F. Peticolas.

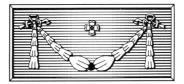

THREE

House and Home

BLACK crape draped the governor's house and Capitol mourning the death of Thomas Jefferson. He had breathed his last as the nation celebrated the fiftieth anniversary of American Independence on July 4, 1826. When, the news from Monticello reached Richmond, surprise and sorrow were universal, and a new generation sensed the irony profoundly.

On July 11, Governor John Tyler, Jr., addressed a large, somber gathering at the Capitol on the subject of Jefferson. At the conclusion, as he descended from the platform he was handed a note advising him that in Massachusetts an aged John Adams had also died on the Fourth of July. Never one to appear overwhelmed, Tyler scribbled hasty sentences on a paper and, standing straight as an arrow, promptly remounted the platform: "Scarcely has the funeral knell of our Jefferson been sounded in our ears," the governor began, "when we are startled by the death-bell of another Patriot—his zealous coadjutor in the holy cause of Revolution . . ."

The governor stood where another hero from that vanished age had addressed cheering, weeping thousands only two years before. Richmond had been swept off its feet by General Lafayette, who stopped through on his American tour. During the American Revolution he had saved the city from the British. The old man declined an invitation to stay at the governor's mansion, perhaps because his entourage was too large, but he dined there on October 27, 1824, with Governor James Pleasants and a large company. Organized public celebrations were held at the Capitol. The square, decorated with giant temporary monuments, was a fitting stage for the indomitable Hero of Two Worlds.

Such were the events of the unfolding 1820s that roused Virginians to ponder their noble past as its recent vestiges slipped away. Politics closed the decade with demands for yet another break with the past, a new constitution for the commonwealth. The year the nation reached fifty the Virginia constitution also was half a century old, and it was loathed by the large new population of the western counties. Agitation to alter it went back many years, and grew so intense that the tidewater had to take heed. The constitutional convention was held at the Capitol from October 1829 to January 1830. Vintage genius was there in abundance. The convention is often described as the last gathering of the Virginia giants. James Madison came down from Montpelier with Dolley, graciously declining Governor William Branch Giles's invitation to "become members of my family, and to accept a chamber in the Government house during the session of the approaching convention." They put up with relatives. James Monroe presided over the first two months of debate, and John Marshall and John Randolph of Roanoke also took part. Governor Giles, although obliged by rheumatism to move about on crutches, played his opposition politics deftly.

At the mansion the door was open all day, the punch bowl filled with spirits for the delegates. Governor Giles carefully mixed the best of Richmond society with his political guests. Evening affairs varied from quiet dinners, sometimes stag, to receptions in the parlor, attended by ladies in great number. A guest at one of the latter wrote in his diary, "The party at the Gov's. was a very large, and very agreeable one. There was a great deal of beauty assembled, perhaps more than I ever saw in one room in Rich[mon]d."

The westerners conceded that the new constitution was an improvement over the old, but a disappointment, too. Representation, and the right to vote, was given to more western counties but the tidewater remained in control. The General Assembly still elected the governor and the office remained weak, although the governor's term was extended to three full years. Old battles had been waged, but ominous questions that divided Virginia along regional lines were in large measure sidestepped. Virginia was a different place in 1830 than it had been in 1820. The old men passing from the scene were being replaced by lesser lights, in times even more trying. Change and turmoil would continue in the thirty years before the Civil War.

Virginia's "state house," or "government house," as the Executive Mansion was often confusingly called in its early period, was the finest official house of any governor in the United States. Some states, Massachusetts, for example, provided apartments for their governors, while others rented houses nearby. When a state built or bought a governor's mansion, the house normally met the philosophical requirement of being roomy but somewhat ordinary. In contrast, the governor's house of Virginia was imposing, set back on its graveled approach, with formal lines of trees planted along the sides. It shared surroundings and stately dignity with the Capitol. Yet the office of governor of Virginia was one of the weakest.

Governor William Branch Giles retired in 1830 not an especially popular governor but a more famous man than when he entered office in 1827. His written opinions against the new constitution, known as the Resolutions of 1827, carried in their time as much weight as had Madison's and Jefferson's Virginia and Kentucky Resolutions, which in 1798 challenged the power of the federal government over individual citizens. An enemy of slavery, Giles also denounced the growing oppression of free blacks in Virginia.

Most of the improvements Governor Giles made to the mansion were to make it more convenient. He introduced running water in a rudimentary way, ordering a spring dug out on the square, lined with stone and connected to the mansion and Capitol through iron pipes. At the mansion a single hydrant was set up in the front yard, where buckets were regularly filled to serve the house, and a supply of water stood ready in case of fire. Inside the house Giles replaced the traditional candlelight in the dining room and parlor with the blaze of light from "smokeless" table lamps with Argand burners, devices that brightened the oil-fueled flame by increasing the flow of oxygen to it. His were fine lamps, encased in gilt brass and cut glass, and were probably set up high on the mantels or on special shelves to shine down in the absence of chandeliers.

John Floyd, who followed Giles in office, was more in step with the political climate of Virginia at the time. In theory an antislavery man, Floyd stood solidly for states' rights. Trained as a medical doctor, he was a graduate of the University of Pennsylvania, but the political life had claimed him early. As governor he hoped to unify the state with internal improvements, especially railroads to link tidewater ports with the Valley. Floyd espoused the nationalism of Henry Clay, and by the time he became governor he had a well-honed hatred for President Andrew Jackson.

Floyd turned more conservative the longer he was governor. To his table at the governor's mansion in early March 1831 came the South Carolinian John C. Calhoun, vice-president of the United States, enemy of President Jackson, and spokesman for states' rights. Floyd invited large groups of men, practically all of them members of the General Assembly, to become acquainted with a man he believed held the nation's future in his hands. In the following summer the governor was confronted with the Southampton slave insurrection led by Nat Turner. Calhoun's worst fears seemed to have been realized.

The rebellion was quickly put down by local militia, but more than fifty persons died in its violence. While Governor Floyd showed no mercy toward Turner and his closest comrades, who were tried and hanged, he did his best to commute the sentences of other participants to being sold or transported out of the country. Floyd may have feared that too many hangings might arouse public indignation and even sympathy. Nat Turner's Rebellion provoked an impassioned debate about slavery in the General Assembly session of 1831-1832, and the experience strongly confirmed Floyd's

Artist John James Audubon visited the Executive Mansion in 1831 and in 1833 while promoting subscriptions to his Birds of America. *He compared his observations with students of nature such as William H. Richardson, superintendent of public buildings, but he drew no birds in Richmond.*

political opinions. To his diary he confided on November 28, 1831, "I am preparing a message to the General Assembly. It will be ultra States Rights."

Governor Floyd entertained frequently at the mansion. He seems to have been on the circuit of prominent travelers, many of whom passed through the Old Dominion during his administration. The naturalist John James Audubon called on him on October 9, 1831. Calhoun returned to the mansion that December, venting his contempt for the tariff bill that the Jacksonians were then sponsoring in Congress. He loudly announced to Floyd and his guests that South Carolina would declare the bill null·and void if it became law. Virginia, he said, should do the same.

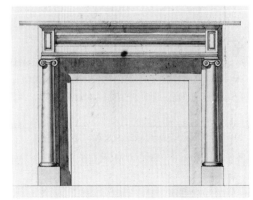

This wash drawing was sent in 1830 from Philadelphia to illustrate the marble mantels and iron grates that were being used for many Virginia houses. Unfortunately, none survives of the three grates and mantels purchased for the mansion.

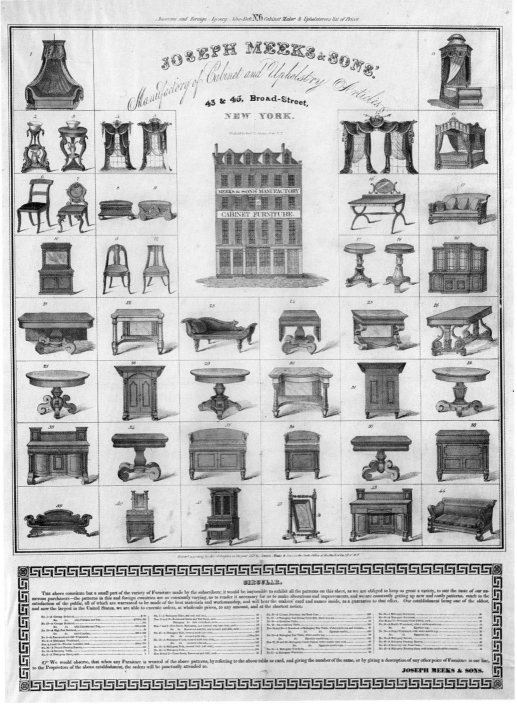

The Metropolitan Museum of Art, gift of Mrs. R.W. Hyde, 1943. (43.15.8)

In 1830 Joseph Meeks and Sons, a famous New York furniture company, shipped several crates of furniture to the Executive Mansion. The shipment included two dozen chairs like the one illustrated at the far left in the third row of the company's colorful advertisement, and two pairs of card tables similar to those in the second row from the bottom.

During the first year of Governor Floyd's administration, the governor's mansion received the finishing touches originally recommended in the commissioners' report of 1813. Outside, the front porch was added, the side porches replaced, and parapets constructed above the eaves. Broken windows were repaired, and the entire exterior was painted for the first time. While furniture was temporarily stored in the Capitol, painters freshened the inside walls, grained the woodwork, and paint-marbled the baseboards. Workmen laid more than four hundred yards of carpeting described as Brussels, extra super, Venetian, and plain blue. Philadelphia firms shipped three marble mantels to be fitted with hobs and grates for the use of coal. Some furniture was repaired, but the schooner *Effort* also brought eight large boxes of furniture from Joseph Meeks and Sons, of New York, including eight tables, several bureaus and wardrobes, and two dozen ornamental mahogany chairs. By October 1830 the *Richmond Whig* could boast that the mansion, "heretofore furnished in a style of inferiority . . . discreditable to Virginia, has, during the summer, been refitted." The exterior had earned "the appellation of elegance," while the interior had been "filled up and furnished with corresponding propriety, and with a union of taste and substantiality."

Even so, as Governor Floyd was leaving office in 1834 he again protested the condition of the house. The General Assembly's appointed commissioners, William Richardson and Blair Bolling, superintendent of public buildings, had made monthly reports of their maintenance at the mansion but because it was considered a private home might have been hesitant to intrude. Life in a governor's mansion can be compared to living over the store or, worse, the office. Places of business are prone to wear and tear that is overlooked in the rush of immediate matters, and the Giles and Floyd administrations had used the house hard. Looking around in some embarrassment, Governor Floyd ordered a massive housecleaning to prepare the mansion for his friend and successor Littleton Waller Tazewell. Carpenters, plasterers, painters, and whitewashers swarmed the building before the close of March 1834.

Governor Tazewell's anti-Jackson stance led him into a controversy with the legislature, and facing an impasse he resigned, after serving only two years. He nevertheless took a real interest in the mansion, as did Ann Nivison Tazewell, the first wife of a governor known actively to have involved herself in decorating the house. They were a devoted couple, married thirty-two years when he was sworn into office; he was fifty-nine and she was soon to be fifty. "With her the throne of human felicity was the family altar. . . . Her heart, like a true Virginia mother she was, was in the midst of her family." Despite the constant interruption of guests, their homelife was close. Six of their eight children had arrived during the first fifteen years of their marriage, but Mary and Ella were still little girls when the Tazewells lived in the mansion. The family read together, gathered in the parlor. Tazewell played chess with the older children.

In the spring of 1834, in the wake of Governor Floyd's housecleaning, Ann Tazewell turned a second army of workmen on the house, and set herself to shopping for things the house needed. First on her list was new china, and she ordered two large tea sets in Richmond through the merchants Allison and Watt, who lent her a set until her shipment arrived. Nearly all her shopping was done in Richmond, where she selected draperies, carpeting, wallpaper, and some furniture from half a dozen household "warehouses."

Privately the Tazewells liked to stay up late and sleep late in the morning. Often the governor lingered over a book, papers, or the chessboard until two or three in the morning. Artificial lighting naturally interested the night-owl governor especially the more general light possible with chandeliers, when all he had were portable candlesticks, oil lamps, and single-light lanterns hanging in the halls. In the autumn of 1835 he ordered the mansion's first chandeliers from C. Cornelius and Son, of Philadelphia. There were two of them, both bronze, with six branches holding sockets for wax candles or lard-oil "peg" lamps. They were suspended by rods from hooks in the ceiling. Prisms refracted each flame many times, causing light to reflect from the mirrors and the whitewashed ceilings. The parlors' new overhead lighting was something rarely seen except in public meeting places and the finest houses.

Tazewell embarked upon some construction projects. A new carriage house went up in 1835 to serve in addition to the one that was there. The trim of the house was repainted and its twelve decorative panels repaired again. Repairs to the outside of the house were almost constant, and the bills that survive in the archives suggest that Mrs. Tazewell spent most of her two years in the mansion conducting work on the inside as well.

The governor's resignation seemed imminent for many months before it finally occurred. A Jacksonian majority in the General Assembly passed legislation ordering Virginia's senators to seek a revocation of the censure of President Jackson issued by the United States Senate in 1834. This law raised the complex constitutional issue of the right of state legislatures to give instructions to their senators. The anti-Jackson Tazewell challenged the assembly's action and, rather than transmit the instructions, resigned after the close of the legislative session in March 1836. Wyndham Robertson, senior member of the Council of State, filled Tazewell's office for the rest of his term.

Soil exhaustion and an ebbing away of population into newer states brought a general economic decline to the commonwealth in the 1830s and 1840s. The old settled areas of Virginia came to be seen as regions past their

prime. An aristocratic history was often recalled through once-grand Virginia houses of the sort described in John Pendleton Kennedy's *Swallow Barn,* published in 1832. The bitter poverty symbolized by crumbling mansions was real. Politics responded with increasing tension between the geographical regions of the state, the young and vigorous opposing the old and spent. Internal improvements, public education, and other positive endeavors common in other states fell short in Virginia.

Unrest was also felt at the governor's house. David Campbell lived there for an uneventful three-year term during which he obtained permission to use an office in the Capitol and to graze a cow in Capitol Square. His successor, Thomas Walker Gilmer, came to office in March 1840 and resigned a year later when the legislature declined to back him in an extradition controversy with New York. Three members of the Council of State—John Mercer Patton and John Rutherfoord from Richmond, and John Munford Gregory from James City County—completed the balance of Gilmer's term but did not occupy the mansion. With the end of Gregory's acting governorship, the legislature began electing governors to serve from January to January—as suggested by the Constitution of 1830 and required by the Constitution of 1851—instead of to March.

Governor James McDowell, inaugurated in the bitter January of 1843, entered office with strong ambitions and high hopes of bringing order after the chaos of the previous few years. This was not to be, except for a very short time at the beginning of his administration, for he too had his conflicts with the General Assembly and was never forgiven for berating the lawmakers for Virginia's shortcomings, such as the "perverted" condition of education in the commonwealth. He worked for internal improvements such as the James River and Kanawha Canal, and took his ideas to the people in orations, but his lack of decisiveness finally turned the public against him.

McDowell was described as a "tall, large, fine looking man, with a bland, winning countenance, and a voice which, though not loud or deep-toned, is nevertheless pleasant and agreeable." His wife was his first cousin, Susanna Smith Preston, grandniece of Patrick Henry. Their daughter, one of ten children, remembered of her mother that "amid the engrossments of a thousand cares at the Government House, she made leisure, outside the run of her ordinary charities, to listen to other calls of piety and philanthropy."

The McDowells entertained hospitably, with one innovation: no liquor. The governor was a temperance man, and the punch bowl in the dining room dried up, spawning jokes in the Capitol about how his popularity had dried up accordingly. Dinners were served using Mrs. Tazewell's fine china as well as several new services and the silver plate accumulated over the years by mansion occupants. The Tazewell chandeliers were traded in for new ones with Argand burners. Heretofore the revolutionary device in lighting had only been used in the mansion in table lamps, of which there were five or six, easily knocked over when the governor's parlor and dining room were filled with people. The chandeliers hanging high overhead were safe. Had it not been for the terrible stench of the oil fumes and occasional dripping, they could have been considered perfect. The McDowells also purchased additional table lamps and mounted a new hanging light in the entrance hall, rigged with pulleys and green cord for easy access. All this suggested more evening activity, just as several other touches, the parlor's new crimson damask curtains, the dining room's gilt porcelain fruit baskets, and even the ice cream freezer and pyramid mold hinted at elegance and social activity, indications of McDowell's optimism in his first months in office.

Considering the high cost of maintaining his official residence, Governor McDowell welcomed a new law in 1843 and probably played a part in getting it through the General Assembly. On March 27, the legislature authorized the use of "the slave convicts" from the state penitentiary to work around the mansion and on the square. This free use of prisoners did not rest well with everyone, for the act was amended the following February to require the governor to pay the penitentiary for these services. The convicts' tasks are carefully described in these laws as applying to the maintenance and improvements of the buildings and grounds. No mention is made of convicts being employed as servants in the governor's house, but in years to come they would perform routine cleaning duties.

If Governor McDowell's three years represented only a futile effort to bring a sinking state to its feet, the administration of William ("Extra Billy") Smith, who followed him, enjoyed fairly universal public approbation and saw at least beginnings of an economic leveling off for Virginia. Smith began his first term as governor on January 1, 1846, as the United States moved toward war with Mexico, and eighteen years later he would return again to serve as the commonwealth's last governor during the Civil War. Smith's nickname came from his early career as a federal mail contractor on the route between Washington, D.C., and Milledgeville, Georgia. Bonuses were paid to reward contractors who extended their lines. So aggressive was William Smith in the pursuit of these extra fees that the elder politicians dubbed him "Extra Billy."

Tall and handsome, he was an amiable character whose taste for the rough-and-tumble of politics had begun in his youth. His popularity beyond the mountains had first developed during short terms in Congress and the General Assembly. Audiences liked his blustery self-assuredness, the wit and charm that came through in his long and vigorous orations. For all the pressures put upon him, he adamantly refused to run for governor. On the day after election day 1845 he arrived home in Warrenton from court in Prince William and was walking down the main street with his saddlebags over his shoulder when a friend called out "Governor Smith!" The legislature had elected him in his absence.

He held back at first, fearing that his purse could not bear the high cost of being governor. "It was a severe trial to me," he wrote of the surprise election. "I determined to decline the position." His political supporters descended upon him, arguing that his refusal would only "delight" his enemies and "deeply mortify" the friends who had "staked themselves" on the advantages to come from his election. "Suffice it to say," wrote Extra Billy Smith, "I yielded to my friends and became Virginia's Governor. How I bore myself is a matter of history, to which I fearlessly refer the curious."

The forty-eight year-old Smith lived on his earnings as a lawyer and the slim profits of farms inherited by his wife, Elizabeth Bell. He was a fine courtroom lawyer, but he also spent money very freely. Governor Smith's spending habits transferred readily to official policy. At the governor's house, his alterations were so extensive that to make way he vacated the place for about four months during the summer of 1846. He spent generously not only on the mansion but also on Capitol Square, which underwent improvements that included some grading and paving, and an ambitious program of planting ornamental trees.

The Smiths fairly filled the house to its rafters. Besides the governor and Mrs. Smith and the seven children there were always long-staying guests from Warrenton and the counties of King George and Culpeper. The Smiths had lost four children in infancy but the seven who survived ranged in age from little Mary Amelia to the twins, William Henry and Caleb, aged twenty-three. The storeroom over the entrance hall became the fifth bedroom. Smith's slaves lived in the second-floor rooms over the kitchen house and laundry, as had other servants serving the mansion before them. Quarters for the coachman and grooms were over the stables, wooden structures that became more than ever the focus of mansion life because Extra Billy and his sons were impassioned horsemen. At the table Elizabeth Smith sometimes threw up her hands in mock exasperation, exclaiming that she would listen to no more talk of horses.

Wishing to make the mansion fit his family, Extra Billy made more numerous changes to the house than anyone who had lived there before, spending three substantial appropriations in a short time. By March 1846 the governor was already giving orders to workmen. Where commissioners had managed most projects before, Extra Billy attended to his personally. On the exterior he did extensive work to one of the porticoes, involving four "fluted columns, caps and abacus." He roofed with tin the old brick walkway that connected house and kitchen, giving it wooden post supports and a combination of lattice and louvered blinds to protect it from blowing rains.

Smith enlarged the interior's livable space by expanding it down into the

Asher Benjamin's American order, a popular Greek Revival adaptation of the Doric, was chosen for the side porches of the mansion.

*John J. Porter's portrait of Gover-
nor William ("Extra Billy")
Smith, who served as governor
from 1846 to 1849 and from 1864
to 1865, hangs in the ballroom of
the Executive Mansion.*

basement. The two rear or east rooms of this "cellar" and the central hall were plastered and wooden floors were laid over the original brick. The dining room was moved below to occupy the space beneath the parlor. He added a second staircase from the main floor, a broad, fine one clearly meant for more visible purposes than the winding service stairs that already stood at the opposite end of the basement hall. In the large pantry, a room next to the service stairs, he installed modern coal-fired ovens.

On the main floor, the former dining room now became the second parlor. A broad opening was cut between it and the old parlor and fitted with sliding doors that opened the two rooms into a long span foreshadowing somewhat today's ballroom. The decor of this double parlor was rich and fashionably "French." Governor Smith ordered a huge mirror from New York—"French plate ornamental," said the bill—and he paid $110. Brussels carpeting wall-to-wall, satin curtains, and "Killarney Fresco" wallpaper formed a background for the new French-style parlor furniture, a mixture of pieces in rosewood, mahogany, and walnut, curved and carved, and deeply cushioned with springs.

The more remarkable of Extra Billy Smith's changes was not this rearrangement and decoration but the installation of indoor toilet and bathing facilities. Some experimental installation of water closets may have already taken place in the fall of 1845, but the work in 1846 was extensive and permanent. Previously the household had used portable "crockery" in the bedrooms and a necessary, or privy, at the rear of the service yard. The steep incline on which the mansion was built lent itself well to a gravity plumbing system, and the house was conveniently downhill from the spring in Capitol Square. There had been a hydrant near the front yard since 1827. Records show the presence of some plumbing inside the house by the mid-1840s, perhaps faucets in the kitchen and the basement pantry.

The toilet room Governor Smith built was more like an indoor privy than a modern bathroom. It was located in one of the two corner rooms in the front of the basement. Against one wall was a wooden "riser," like a stairstep, upon which two seats were mounted concealing bowls, pipes, and the like. The water tanks for the two toilets were overhead; when a crank was turned, a stream of water rushed down the pipe, through the bowl, and in an unhalting flow continued outside either into an underground receptable of brick, or onto an open-air waste ground along Governor Street. Decorators and painters Dogget and Anderson, employed by the general contractor William Forbes, finished the room by building up the floor to allow space for the pipes and sheathing the walls with pine, grained with paint in the mansion's oak pattern. A "shower bath" also was built in the basement with a "copper rose," or shower head, and a lever to release the flow from the reservoir above.

The installation in 1846 of a partial central heating system required cutting into the walls and must account for the large order of plastering and wallpapering done on the main and second floors that year. The new furnace was situated in the smallest basement room beneath the entrance hall, and its "pipes," or ducts, extended to the principal rooms. Nothing much is known about this furnace except that it was relatively cheap to construct. A gravity system, it modestly supplemented the coal fires in the

SHOWER BATHS!

We would invite the attention of the public to an improved and very superior SHOWER BATH—specimens of which may now be seen at our store.

No family or individual should be without one of these Baths, at once so promotive of both comfort and health.

We respectfully suggest an early call and orders before the warm weather sets in.

For sale by
WM. F. BUTLER & CO, 79, Main street, sign of Gilt Pitcher.

March 22

Virginia State Library and Archives
In March 1847, two months after the state paid for the installation of a shower in the basement of the Executive Mansion, this advertisement for a "shower bath" appeared in the Richmond Enquirer.

fireplaces, providing breaths of warm air for those human parts not facing the hot glow from the hearth.

The major event of Governor Smith's administration was the war with Mexico from 1846 to 1848. News of President James K. Polk's war message and the ensuing declaration in May flooded the streets of Richmond with citizens hot for a fight. Young men from all over the state swelled the ranks of the Richmond Blues, the Richmond Grays, the Rangers, the Marshall Guard, and the Fayette Artillery. Representatives sent to Washington met with the president and offered Virginia's services, which were at last called for in November. Governor Smith asked the people of Virginia and the General Assembly to outfit the volunteers with uniforms, arms, and ammunition until such time as the United States Army took over.

It was an exciting time for the city and for the governor's house, although the mansion seems not to have been central to the festival of preparation and celebration that accompanied the military send-off to the Mexican War. Governor Smith's hospitality was well known, but the most notable activities, the dinners, the balls, all took place downtown in hotels, usually by subscription, with the governor and his wife as guests. The first of the volunteers left in January 1847, followed by the remainder in February.

Their remarkable successes led to many illuminations of the Capitol, governor's mansion, and business district. The volunteers who stayed home marched frequently on Capitol Square. Notable victories were honored with cannon salutes that invariably shattered windows in the mansion, but then, celebrations on the square always had—every year on the great holidays of January 8, February 22, and the Fourth of July.

President Polk came to town. The governor met with him, but not at the mansion. The house was more for business than ceremony. Business callers seated themselves in chairs along the walls of the entrance hall and were less than decorous. Important visitors were hurried past them into the little parlor on the front of the house, or, if they were family friends, into the large double parlors at the back, where the sofas were the most comfortable. Washstands in the principal rooms offered the convenience of hand and face washing, and six spittoons facilitated a popular male pastime probably practiced in every room of the main floor, on any day of any week, all year long.

The coming of peace in 1848 set off an explosion of merrymaking and honoring. If the war had turned sour to others, Virginians had reason to celebrate both success and good luck. Casualties were relatively few. Most of the fighting men came home, sunburned and triumphant. Heroic generals passed through town to claim a laurel or two, Zachary Taylor, Winfield Scott, John Anthony Quitman, and James Shields.

Extra Billy Smith's role in the Mexican War was slight. Having praised the warriors and supported the war in every way he could, the governor left

TO THE RICHMOND LIGHT INFANTRY BLUES.

This plate is most respectfully dedicated

R. A. Brock.

by Huddy & Duval

Maximilian Godefroy's formal landscape was the background of this military scene in Capitol Square on the eve of the Mexican War.

office on New Year's Day 1849. The war had opened up to settlement a part of the continent previously unavailable, bad news again for Virginia. As Smith had feared, he had been seriously damaged financially during three years in the "government house." The twins, William Henry and Caleb, had headed west when they heard about the fabulous discoveries in California. Extra Billy, his legal practice stagnant, his debts large, soon followed, to try and restore his fortune in places where gold lay in the streets.

These years saw energy renewed in the commonwealth through improved agricultural production and some industry. No boom came about, but the good signs gave hope that maybe good times were returning. Sectional issues north and south dominated national politics, and in Virginia were paralleled in the continuing east-west controversies. The national problem had temporary relief in the Compromise of 1850, and Virginia found hers in a new constitutional convention. Railroads, canals, and the appearance of industry had brought changes to all of Virginia, but the majority now lived to the west, which included present-day West Virginia.

The convention was held in the Capitol, like that twenty years before. Governor John Buchanan Floyd, son of the earlier Governor Floyd, played only a minor role, limited more by his inclination than his position. The westerners were heard, and, while the constitution that emerged after long months might have been more extreme had it been left entirely in their hands, they had their way in many particulars. Notably, the Constitution of 1851 extended the governor's term from three to four years.

Governor John Buchanan Floyd's tenure might be seen as the last of the palmy days. Virginians were experiencing enough new prosperity to feel good about themselves. Extra Billy Smith's limited program for landscaping in Capitol Square was expanded in 1851 when the Richmond city council engaged John Notman, of Philadelphia, architect and designer of Richmond's beautiful Hollywood Cemetery, to create a new master plan for the square, replacing the severely formal lines of Godefroy with a scheme in the fashionable "rural" style. Convict laborers reduced the steep hillside southwest of the Capitol. Large sums were spent acquiring native trees and shrubbery "to render the Square a place of delightful resort." Young trees along the walks of the square—maple, ash, tulip poplar, dogwood, cedar, and holly—were boxed for protection four or five feet up from the ground. John Morton, the first professional gardener ever hired for the mansion and square, was followed late in 1851 by Charles A. Ruhle. Two greenhouses built near the stable buildings had slanted glass roofs and, inside, long stepped tables for hundreds of clay flower pots.

In the summer of 1851 the *Richmond Daily Times* reported that "the Armory Brass Band gave their first soiree on the Capitol Square Tuesday

To prepare Capitol Square for the planned monument to Washington, early in the 1850s Philadelphia architect John Notman designed a new landscaping scheme with gentle undulations and curving walks in the fashionable picturesque style. Notman adapted the site's natural features to its man-made monuments, making Capitol Square the first large urban park in America to employ the picturesque rural style.

evening. The turn out was pretty general, and all present seemed delighted with the excellent music discoursed by the band. We were glad to see a large number of ladies present, and trust they will continue to encourage, by their presence, these pleasant entertainments. By doing so, they will promote health, refine the public taste, develop the social feeling, freshen the spirits and increase the happiness of the population.''

Already work had begun on the great Washington statue, its mighty granite foundation rising obstructively in the middle of Godefroy's long, straight tree-lined road that ran from the western gate of the square to the governor's mansion. A national competition had yielded a winning design for the monument by the American sculptor Thomas Crawford, who lived in Rome. The model, on display in the Capitol, showed George Washington on horseback atop a tall pedestal, surrounded by six Virginia heroes of the American Revolution. Ten thousand people had come to watch the elaborate cornerstone laying, climaxed by an address by President Zachary Taylor, a native son, who said he felt "as a child returning to his parents."

It was time, too, for good works at home. Sally Buchanan Preston Floyd busied herself adding to what Governor Smith had bought for the mansion. By carriage she traveled to the stores of Richmond, selecting china, glassware, linen yard goods and drapery material and fringe. She worked closely with Captain Charles Dimmock, who replaced Blair Bolling as the official in charge of the public buildings. When time came to buy furniture, Mrs. Floyd seems to have asked that Mrs. Dimmock do the choosing and dispatched her to Alexandria to the Green family furniture factory on South Fairfax Street. Mrs. Dimmock bought clever "vis a vis" or double chairs and two "conversation" chairs, all upholstered in crimson plush. In Richmond shops Sally Floyd selected "fine satin ceiling paper," oak-panel wallpaper, a "crumb brush," and a breakfast bell. Invoices occasionally written to "Lady Floyd" must be interpreted as respect on the part of the merchants and not a poke at her manner.

The "bathing room" or shower bath in the basement was expanded nicely to include a bathtub. Originally a room meant probably for the use of men, its convenience and decoration perhaps expanded its clientele to include the ladies who usually bathed in portable tubs in their bedrooms. Here was a copper tub, and a china sink with marble surround. Fancy oilcloth, a kind of early-day linoleum, protected the wooden floor from splashing and wet feet. The woodwork was oak grained and the walls papered. If the bathing room had a boiler or hot water heater, the fact is not recorded, but there was a fireplace where bathwater could be warmed by the potful, the old way, to take the chill off that drawn from the tap.

Looking over the numerous records of Floyd purchases for the mansion one hurries past the monotony of china and glassware and sofas and chairs. Screen doors catch the eye as do garden sprinklers, and the new kitchen range. The heating system was improved. Gas-lighting was installed on the main floor. In such innovations one senses a strong rhythm of progress through the years at the mansion. And Governor Floyd's was a peaceful time compared to the times to come.

Museum of the Confederacy, gift of Mr. & Mrs. Orme Wilson, Jr., in memory of the Honorable and Mrs. Orme Wilson. Acc. no. 988.14.1. Photograph by Katherine Wetzel.

This rosewood étagère, one of a pair, was purchased for the mansion in 1855 from a Philadelphia cabinetmaking firm. The invoice described the new furniture for the parlor, hall, and dining room as "French," then the latest fashion in American furniture and decorating taste. Sold at an auction in the 1880s, several pieces remained in Virginia and were recently donated to the Museum of the Confederacy.

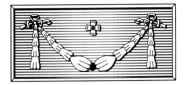

FOUR

Antebellum Days

RICHMOND, largest of the southern state capitals in the 1850s, had a flavor quite its own. The glories of its drawing rooms and of its hotels and horse races were equally proclaimed. Planters came in from the country to taste city pleasures and buy things. Dickens and Thackeray adorned its platforms and enjoyed its hot spoon bread, its salty ham, its cold mint juleps. Richmond citizens paid big prices to hear Jenny Lind, the Swedish Nightingale, and flattered all the great actors of the day with packed houses. They also crowded around by the thousands to watch hangings at the penitentiary at no cost. Fine carriages mingled with humble carts in the dirt-and-gravel streets. Most of the thirty thousand residents walked. Unremarkable commercial and manufacturing districts near the James River and Shockoe Creek were surrounded by residential neighborhoods on higher ground, some of them handsome, slumbering among shade trees.

For all its charm, however, Richmond, like the other earlier-settled parts of the state, was retreating more and more into itself. Intellectually, highpoints might be found in a certain awareness of the finer things of life. But that peculiar feature of southern life, slavery, ever required greater explanation, and, when the justifications proved unsatisfactory, reason yielded to passionate, blind defensiveness. In the decade before the Civil War the dilemma over slavery loomed so large in Virginia that it was to dominate all else, until visitors from outside who had once felt an immediate kinship with these warm, gay people saw themselves as aliens who dared not comment other than flatteringly on what they saw.

The lofty roost of Capitol Square provided one of Richmond's most memorable views. Alexander MacKay, a Canadian journalist, strolled about the square in the antebellum era, admiring the mansion and mounting the portico of the Capitol. He found the view in the antebellum era "both extensive and varied. In the immediate foreground is the town, the greater portion of which is so directly underneath you that it almost seems as if you could leap into it. Before you is the James River, tumbling in snowy masses over successive ledges of rock, its channel being divided by several islands,

GOVERNORS HOUSE

One of ten vignettes around the edge of the 1853 Smith map of Henrico County, this engraving verifies such details of the mansion's architectural ornament as the plaster festoons in the recessed panels and the decorative molding within the solid sections of the parapet.

which are shrouded in foliage, and imbedded in foaming rapids. To the south of the river, an extensive vista opens up, spreading far to the right and left, cleared in some places, but, generally speaking, mantled in the most luxuriant vegetation."

"The scene," he continued, "is one over which the stranger may well linger, particularly on a bright summer's day, when his cheek is fanned by the cooling breezes, which come gaily skipping from the distant Alleghenies, carrying the fragrant perfume of the magnolia and honeysuckle on their wings, and his spirit is soothed by the incessant murmur of the rapids, which from the height at which he stands, steals gently to his ear." The governor's mansion enjoyed some of these views from its tall south and east windows. Forever embraced by the winds, it was a house not yet forty years old. Families had moved in and out, leaving scars. It was not the finest house in Richmond by any measure, but, while being the capital's first citizen brought only transitory honor to the governors, their office brought permanent distinction to the house.

The gubernatorial election of 1851 was the first in which Virginians cast their own ballots to determine who would live in the governor's house. Ironically, the winner was a native of Orange County, New York, who had come to Virginia at fifteen. Governor Joseph Johnson was, moreover, a man from the west—present-day West Virginia—put into office by western voters. "Governor Johnson," wrote a personal friend, "was emphatically a man of the people."

The westerners considered him their man, but with mediocre support in the legislature his was a troubled administration. Determined to pull Virginia's economic ox out of the ditch, the small, black-eyed Johnson took a hard look at the commonwealth's development in comparison to other states, particularly in New England. Virginia, he concluded, fell far short in business, agriculture, education, and the general well-being of its people. As a beginning, the westerner wanted a hastened pace of internal improvements, better to bind together his state's disparate regions. While accusing him of being partisan, the legislature nevertheless funded his railroad program. To eastern politicans who took exception to his negative remarks about Virginia, he argued, "Virginia has greatly the advantage over any portion of the North in all the elements requisite to constitute a commercial and prosperous community," but "like the unfaithful servant" in the Bible "she has failed to improve the talent entrusted to her care." Denounced in the eastern press, the governor was acclaimed, for the most part, in the west. Backed into a fighting stance, he soon found his political situation tense.

Johnson's prestige suffered permanent damage early in his administration with the Jordan Hatcher affair, in which he commuted to sale and

The entry hall

transportation the death sentence of a teenage slave who had murdered his cruel factory supervisor. The immediate public reaction was hostile. "Come one, come all," beckoned the *Richmond Republican*, "and protect your firesides by putting down all those who uphold murder." On May 7, 1852 more than a thousand people gathered at the city hall to demand the execution of Jordan Hatcher, and soon enough the crowd worked itself into a mob that flowed on to Capitol Square, gaining new recruits. Pushing through the iron gates of the square, they stood before the governor's house with torches, "shouting and hissing and cursing," calling the governor out again and again. Johnson did not respond, but remained inside in the gaslight, surrounded by friends who urged him in vain to flee through the stable yard. After pelting the house with rocks and breaking windows, the crowd, unchallenged, finally departed. Jordan Hatcher was saved, for the governor did not yield. The episode bared for a moment the anger that lay just beneath the apparently tranquil surface of Virginia in the 1850s.

The Johnsons led a relatively quiet private life at the mansion. They draped the house in black when Henry Clay died, and they observed punctually all other ceremonial efforts the job of governor required, although these were few. Deeply religious people, Joseph and Sarah Johnson devoted time to the Baptist church and held religious meetings at home. Their other social activities usually were small dinners for delegates and visiting friends from across the mountains. Richmond society had no use for them, nor they for it. Married almost fifty years at the time he became governor, the Johnsons had a large family of grown children all settled elsewhere. A son Henry managed the large family farm in Harrison County.

The new governor sworn in on New Year's Day 1856 was quite different from the outgoing Joseph Johnson. Henry Alexander Wise was a public man, not one, like Johnson, to live in quiet seclusion with his philosophies. Wise's views crossed all party lines. An old-time Jacksonian, in a sense, with occasional liberal ideas, he had also been a Whig, but on the subject of slavery he was vociferously southern. In the fifties the institution of slavery and its perpetuation became almost an obsession with him, hence his political popularity in the tidewater. As a public speaker he was a showman. John Quincy Adams wrote in his diary of one of Wise's speeches to Congress that the Virginian "disgorged a whole cargo of filthy invective" for three hours running.

Tall and bony, Wise, an Accomack County native, stood about six feet and weighed about one hundred thirty-five pounds. His hair was thick and coarse, long to his shoulders and brushed back over his big ears with no attempt at style, and in the wind, looked wild, like Andrew Jackson's, only it was dark auburn instead of white and in sunlight seemed frequently to change its tones of red. He did not smile much. A very large mouth and a big nose were set off by tallow-colored flesh. Gray eyes tinged with blue riveted on a fellow human with unblinking tenacity. From such a description he might have seemed a comic character, yet he appeared anything but foolish. Governor Wise had presence: in a crowded room he stood out as one to be reckoned with.

Mary Elizabeth Lyons, of Richmond, was the governor's third wife and stepmother to his children, two of whom were grown and no longer at home. The youngest boy, John Sargeant Wise, remembered first seeing the mansion on a snowy January 8, 1856, by coincidence it was also a national holiday, celebrated less and less frequently as the anniversary of Andrew Jackson's victory at New Orleans forty years before. Johnny Wise recalled moving into "a fine old structure, simple in exterior, very capacious," that made the house on his father's plantation look by comparison like a "wren-box," at least to his youthful eyes.

His family had been crushed by his mother's death. On the plantation Johnny Wise had lived with little control, until his father's remarriage after which "Miss Mary" put everything back in order. Johnny Wise later remembered Mary Wise tenderly as "refined and cultivated," with a "most lovable disposition." She had taught him "to observe mealtimes; to appear with hair brushed and face and hands washed; to attend family prayers," and to study and become more orderly in his habits. "All which came in good time," he wrote, for with his father's election he "was soon to become a city boy."

The election had been heated. Feverous nativism peaked in the sensational Know-Nothing party, which gained a large following in Virginia. The fires kindled by the debates over the Kansas-Nebraska Act of 1854 had by no means subsided. Politics was the center of all attention, and Wise scampered into office on the ticket of the new Democratic party. An emotional electorate wrote Wise's name on the great majority of ballots, amid many controversies. To heighten the excitement, the new governor was considered an important contender for the Democratic nomination for president of the United States. This prospect brought greater public attention to the governor's mansion than the house had ever known before.

Because many years later John Sargeant Wise was to write a memoir, *The End of An Era*, we know considerable about life in the governor's house during his father's term from 1856 to 1860. Father, stepmother, and most of the children lived there, attended by house slaves from the plantation, who were presided over by the butler Jim. The governor was a temperance man who grudgingly accepted the serving of liquor to guests as a political necessity. "I find my office no sinecure," he complained soon after moving to the mansion. At his first reception "the whole city rushed my liquor so free that the footing of the bill frightens me." In spite of his hospitality, he made no secret of his feeling against drinking. "I have been a candidate three times for the suffrages of the people in the oldest district of 'Old Virginia,' proverbial for *honey drams, mint juleps, hail storms, slings, dew drops*, and every description of nectared drink, and have never found it necessary, or requisite, to obtain a single vote, to resort to the vulgar graces of the familiar cup." But the punch bowl at the mansion remained in place while the General Assembly was in session.

Private routine for the family was not entirely different from what they had enjoyed on the farm, except that everybody usually left home at some point during the day. The ladies went calling after breakfast nearly every weekday, the governor spent time at the Capitol, and the children went to school. Only two full meals were served, breakfast rather late, and an abundant and leisurely "dinner" at about 3 P.M. Home from an evening drive at about 7:30 P.M. they were greeted with the equivalent of a substantial tea in the parlors, sandwiches made with leftover meats or homemade preserves and a variety of light dishes. The food was passed on trays or arranged on the center table where everybody helped themselves and ate from tea tables before their chairs. These little Chinese painted tables did not fold, but were designed to "nest," or stack, when not in use. Company was often invited to share the parlor supper, for which governor and family dressed in their best.

While Wise was not a rich man, he spent money as though he were, giving dinners at the governor's mansion. He may have believed it necessary, considering the stormy times and his national ambitions, as a means of keeping in touch with what people were thinking. The basement dining room where the dinners were held seated thirty-six and was fitted up nicely with a marble mantel on the coal-burning fireplace, two glass-shaded gas chandeliers, a crowd of walnut and mahogany furniture, and sweet-smelling straw matting laid wall-to-wall.

The governor's only vice was tobacco, which he smoked or chewed constantly. His office was a den of tobacco stench. Spittoons were kept in the parlors, dining room, and bed chambers, and the entrance hall was no exception. On most days it was as crowded as a courthouse lobby. Governor Wise's callers sat in Gothic-style chairs made of oak and covered in morocco, idly perusing newspapers or legal papers and smoking and chewing and spitting until the secretary beckoned them for their turn in the office. Up the stairs and beyond closed doors were the family quarters, quiet, dusted, and polished, as different as sun and moon from the domain of the rest. Such was the contrast of life in this public house.

For Johnny Wise the mansion and Capitol Square were paradise. The Wises were the only residents of the square. Delegates, guards, and officials of government left at the close of day. As a grown man John Sargeant Wise recalled an idyllic boyhood on the square, where so many adults took special notice of him: "Young gentlemen of nine years of age are not apt to underestimate their own importance in such a situation, and I was no exception." The country lad's only complaint was his cool reception by the neighborhood boys. All were "cats," members of neighborhood gangs from each of Richmond's hills. The boys liked to play on Capitol Square but treated the governor's son as an outcast.

Johnny Wise and his elder brother Richard had their share of fights with the Richmond boys, whose fathers were often Know-Nothings and hated the governor. Longing to be accepted as cats, they became bored by the mansion, its "play-grounds, and stables, and conservatory, and outhouses." Their lone companion, Marion Dimmock, son of the superintendent of public buildings, felt likewise rejected, but being resourceful and well inside the temples of power the boys soon devised a plan for turning the tables.

Captain Charles Dimmock was also head of the Public Guard. His son and the Wise boys persuaded him to establish a boys' guard, complete with uniforms. Governor Wise responded to this good idea by having a hundred old muskets cut down to size for this "Guard of the Metropolis." New memberships lay entirely in the boys' hands, and elections were unhurried amid a full schedule of weekly drilling, regular and visible. Envious cats

Virginia State Library and Archives
John Sargeant Wise, son of Gov-
ernor Henry Wise, was too
young to carry a musket in the
boys' guard when he moved to
the mansion in 1856, but by May
1864 he was old enough to fight
with the VMI cadets in the battle
of New Market, where he was
wounded. Wise carried Lee's
final wartime dispatch from
Farmville to Jefferson Davis in
Danville, served in Congress,
and was defeated by Fitzhugh
Lee in the election of 1885.

pressed to the iron fence to watch the drills, longing for a uniform, a musket, and the thrill of the march. The boys' guard grew selectively, and Johnny Wise no longer lacked for playmates.

By the late 1850s much of the improvement on the grounds of Capitol Square was complete—the walks, the promenades. Several nights a week a military band played concerts there. Large crowds collected at about dusk for the music, and walked about. With the help of wooden bollards, about the size of fire plugs, the square was restricted to pedestrians, but through some failure in planning the posts were set too close together to allow passage of the fashionable new hoopskirts. Women protested, and gateways were made.

During the concerts it was often made known among the governor's friends that the mansion would be open, after the music ended. Darkness had fallen by then. Gaslight illuminated the crimson parlors, shone on the rose-scattered Brussels carpet, and glowed in the mirrors. While Governor Wise's daughters played the Chickering piano in one parlor, the governor held court in the second. Waiters passed punch and sweets. Sugared fruit was a specialty in season. Ice cream and cake were always in demand. In the basement the long oval dining-room table was covered with starched white damask and filled with good things to eat.

The Wises rejoiced when the governor's eldest son, Jennings, came home from Europe, where he had served as secretary to the American legations in Berlin and Paris. He hoped to give his services to his father's presidential bid, and when that came to nothing he decided to stay anyway. Jennings Wise, twenty-five, had lived in Europe since his teens. Educated to be a lawyer, he was clever, charming, and handsome, and he became the lion of every drawing room in Richmond. In the room he shared with Johnny, he opened his steamer trunks to reveal stylish coats, breeches, shirts, and hats, boots, jewelry, and photographic pictures. The little brother, smitten by the brilliance of this half brother he had never seen before, imitated him in every way he could. In the politically electric atmosphere Jennings soon turned from law to journalism, and blazed in sharp-tongued glory as editor of the *Richmond Enquirer.*

The governor and Johnny vied for Jennings's time. Jennings took long walks with his father, and sat for hours talking and listening in the mansion office. With Johnny he liked to live up to his legend and recount stories of his school days in Germany. His romantic nature took flight in religion and notions of chivalry. As a student he had learned to respect the code duello as the honorable way to settle private differences. During the two years he lived in the governor's house he fought eight duels, not with the sword, as he had in Germany, but with pistols. Johnny, too, became fascinated with dueling, and Jennings ordered the silhouette of a man cut out in wood, full-size, which he set up as a target in the stable yard and used to practice his own

Virginia State Library and Archives
Obadiah Jennings Wise, the
dashing eldest brother of John
Sargeant Wise, returned from
Europe when their father
became governor. Jennings's
romantic ideas about dueling,
religion, and politics inspired
blind admiration in young
Johnny. As a controversial news-
paper editor, Jennings fought
eight duels in two years. He died
in battle during the Civil War.

dueling and to teach Johnny. When John Wise remembered this episode as a mature man, he reflected in astonishment that such a thing could have taken place.

During October 1855 the first two statues for the great Washington monument group arrived in Richmond. Then in early November 1857, Crawford's equestrian statue of George Washington was unloaded at the docks and pulled by horses as far as Main Street, where the horses gave out. More than a thousand men and boys, "the male population of the city," recalled Johnny Wise, then took on the task, towing and pushing the heavy load all the way to Capitol Square. Several months were spent in setting the main statue and the smaller ones of Henry and Jefferson on the granite pedestal. The day of the unveiling, February 22, 1858, produced rain, snow, and hail. Mud was deep in the streets. A program of oratory and marching militia was climaxed by an evening of illumination throughout the main parts of the city, including the square.

Public receptions at the mansion were not common, and must have contrasted sharply to the smaller occasions after the concerts. The record is vague as to how these free-for-all open houses were managed, but it is fairly certain that the basement dining room was not used, because of the size of the crowds. Captain Dimmock supervised the removal of some of the

The timbers and rope in this 1858 photograph raised Thomas Crawford's equestrian statue of Washington onto its pedestal. Rings forged to the saddle were supposed to support the entire statue, but a skeptical Charles Dimmock, superintendent of public buildings, placed a rope cushioned by a mattress under the horse. His precaution averted tragedy, for when the statute was lifted, a ring snapped.

furniture from the two parlors to storage. Thick linen "crash" was laid over the Brussels carpeting to protect it from the feet of perhaps a thousand callers. Refreshments were set out on a table at the end of the south parlor. The governor received in the hall, with the women of the household visible in the little parlor behind him.

Through the last years of the 1850s Governor Wise, a politican of national reputation, was called on more and more as a spokesman for the southern viewpoint. He made frequent public addresses, always in a sense mild-mannered, yet stirring the coals of unrest. During the last year of his administration John Brown's attack on Harpers Ferry made him a household word, a participant in the most emotional event of all those preceding the Civil War.

The governor was awakened from his afternoon nap on Monday, October 17, 1859, with a telegram, and by the time he settled himself downstairs in his office his table was piled with telegrams about the seizure by a party of raiders of the federal armory at Harpers Ferry. He took down the Code of Virginia and, after finding what he needed, sent a telegram to the commandant of the militia at Charlestown. The militia was ordered out. Johnny Wise, hearing the news on the street downtown, hurried home, and stood by his father's office. He remembered how the telegrams kept coming in, "describing a condition of excitement amounting to a panic in the neighborhood of Harper's Ferry."

Later in the day Wise ordered the 1st Virginia Regiment to the railroad depot at 8 P.M. By nightfall the station was swarming with people, both militiamen and civilians. Thousands milled about thickly in the street, awaiting the departure of the train. The governor had left the mansion, Jennings at his side, and joined his cabinet in a makeshift office inside the depot, still receiving telegrams.

By now it was understood that the raid was part of a plot to start a massive liberation of slaves, and the panic heightened. The governor's order was to go by rail to Washington, D.C., then to Harpers Ferry. He intended to go along, and many officials and politicans joined in. Johnny Wise rushed back to the governor's mansion, "donned a little blue jacket with brass buttons," armed himself with a tall Virginia rifle, and "crept into the line of K Company."

As he easily slipped past the guards and onto the train, back at the mansion two of the maids went to Mary Elizabeth Wise and told her that the boy had gone to the train with a rifle. In horror she called the butler, Jim, who hurried to the station, where he told the governor what Johnny had done. "What! Is that young rascal really trying to go?" exclaimed the governor in mock outrage. "Hunt him up, Jim! Capture him! Take away his arms, and march him home in front of you!" A roar of laughter sent Jim off to the train, where, after a chase he collared Johnny and took him home.

*These young soldiers of the 1st Virginia Militia—the Richmond Grays—
brandished their weapons for the photographer as they answered Governor
Wise's call for troops during John Brown's Raid. Although the Grays
reached Harpers Ferry after Brown's capture, they stayed on duty through
his trial and execution. John Wilkes Booth, then a stock actor at the
Richmond Theater, served with the Grays at Harpers Ferry.*

The rest of the John Brown episode is well known. Governor Wise arrived at Harpers Ferry at one in the afternoon on Tuesday, October 18, where he interviewed the captured John Brown, together with some other conspirators. It was his decision that Brown be tried as a sane man, and ultimately he would refuse to commute the sentence of death. Of Brown the governor said: "They are themselves mistaken who take him to be a madman. . . . He is a man of clear head, of courage, fortitude, and simple ingenuousness. He is cool, collected and indomitable. . . . He is a fanatic, vain and garrulous; but firm, truthful and intelligent."

Governor Wise quickly made contact with the man who was to succeed him, John Letcher, and they drew up elaborate plans for a prompt transfer of authority on the last day of 1860, instead of New Year's Day 1861. Bad weather, beginning around Christmas, rendered this impossible, although Letcher's inaugural ceremony was held as planned on December 31 in a fierce snowstorm. He returned with his family to the Exchange Hotel. Wise could not get moved out, nor Letcher in, before January 3. The new governor's years were to be those of the Civil War.

GOVERNORS HOUSE RICHMOND V.A.

Virginia State Library and Archives

Finishing touches added to the Executive Mansion in 1830—the parapet, front porch, and rebuilt side porches—are illustrated in this color lithograph, sold with a similar print of the White House of the Confederacy by Frederick Diehlman during the Civil War. Diehlman's print inaccurately depicts the site, scale, proportions, and windows of the mansion, but nevertheless it was frequently reprinted.

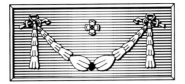

FIVE

Dixie

GOVERNOR John Letcher was a moderate, unlike Governor Wise. Lacking Wise's national political ambitions—which had revived for the presidential election of 1860—Letcher had a consuming interest in his state's politics. He liked the game of the thing more than the prestige. Taking the reins without hesitation, he worked long hours at his new job, filled with hope, though acutely aware of the explosive character of feelings between the North and the South. He asked the federal government for a larger than usual allotment of firearms for the militia. Against heartfelt pleas from the North for clemency, he greased the wheels of justice to hurry the last of John Brown's comrades to the gallows.

His wife and five children moved with him to the governor's house. They found the building in good order. By shifting the partitions over the parlors, space had been created upstairs in 1855 for a second bathroom with copper tub, water closet, lavatory, wooden walls, and an oilcloth on the floor. Susan Mary Holt Letcher, ten years the governor's junior, was a small, pretty woman devoted to her family's well-being. The rough-hewn features of the governor—tall, thin, and sandy haired—were a marked contrast to hers.

He had few cultured refinements and pretended to none. Good-hearted and jovial by nature, Honest John was talkative and witty, and usually won people's affection with ease. His was a close family, and anyone who visited was swept into this friendly·circle. They gathered in the parlors and sang or read aloud. Socially the governor liked to have a good time. Bourbon was his drink, alternated occasionally with white lightning from the city market. A friend back home in Lexington wrote to him, "I have heard some remarks about the free use of whiskey in your office in your Mansion, by your visitors and heard it mentioned by your best friend in this County that he had heard, that you [drank] at your office at the Capitol."

The friend went on to suggest that the traditional mansion punch bowl be put away, that drinks only be served "among private friends in a private room." Letcher was annoyed by the advice, and refused to consider it. He dismissed the stories of his drunkenness as part of the smear campaign against him.

Letcher's biographer, F. N. Boney, wrote that Letcher was "probably the most thoroughly bourgeois chief executive the state had yet known." By his politics still a Jacksonian, he had been elected in the past by Whigs, and now was governor on the Democratic ticket. Secession was the issue of the hour. Only a few days after his swearing in, delegates from other Southern states began to arrive at his door asking for a Southern convention.

These political visits received wide coverage in newspapers north and

Governor John Letcher

south. The governor gave dinners for his guests at the mansion, and saw to it that they met the key figures of the General Assembly, but he wanted no part of secession. Less his opposition than his half-hearted support contributed to the secessionists' initial failure, in the spring of 1860, to push through the General Assembly a call for a state convention. Governor Letcher remained, in his own words, "calm and conservative." Yet moderates lacked the organization and program to combat for long the radical upswing.

Political events moved quickly in the autumn of 1860, but otherwise it was a tranquil, pleasant season, climaxed by the visit of the eighteen-year-old Prince of Wales, the future Edward VII, son of Queen Victoria and great-grandson of George III. The prince declined Governor Letcher's invitation to stay in the governor's mansion, preferring to remain close to his entourage at a hotel. Surrounded in public by thousands of people, the rather homely Prince Albert Edward cut quite a swath through Richmond,

Library of Congress

A panoramic photograph taken by Mathew Brady's photographers after the evacuation fire of 1865 shows this rare view of the rear of the mansion. Capitol Square formed an effective firebreak that protected the Capitol at its center, but the General Courts Building in the southeast corner burned and the Executive Mansion was saved by a bucket brigade laboring on the roof through the night.

as he did everywhere else on his American tour. After viewing Houdon's great statue of Washington in the Capitol, and Crawford's on the square, he called on the governor at the mansion, where Elizabeth Letcher and her close friends waited excitedly in the parlors.

Abraham Lincoln was elected president a month after the royal visit. Governor Letcher's hold on the legislature weakened as the cries for a state convention increased. By the time of the election of delegates, February 4, 1861, South Carolina and six other states had already seceded from the Union. In Texas, Governor Letcher's old friend Sam Houston, also a native of Rockbridge County, Virginia, was removed from the governorship for refusing to go along with secession. Letcher did not want the same fate.

The Virginia convention opened in the Capitol on February 13 with a majority of moderates falling between extremes of ardent secessionists and of Unionists from beyond the mountains. Governor Letcher, laboring against secession, politicked the convention behind the scenes. For a while he set his hopes on the ill-fated peace convention assembled in Washington, then he turned home again to problems on his doorstep. In his office at the mansion he held long meetings and wrote and received a vast correspondence on the events at hand.

The news of Fort Sumter came to Richmond by telegraph on April 12. By dawn the city was in an uproar, the day of the thirteenth a carnival of fireworks and Confederate flags. A great crowd brought several cannons from the arsenal on Cary Street to Capitol Square and fired salutes over the city, then gravitated to the mansion, where they called out the governor. Letcher appeared on the front porch, sadly resigned to the demise of the Union. He gazed at the Confederate flag held up before him and said that he did not recognize it. Virginia was still part of the Union. Over the crowd's hissing and booing the governor said that he would cast his lot with his state, whatever her course might be.

On April 15 President Lincoln called for 75,000 state militia to put down the rebellion. Resistance to secession evaporated and on April 17 the convention voted to secede. The governor laid aside his efforts for peace, and set himself to work harder at the task of increasing Virginia's military forces and supplies. Letcher listened to advice, but planned his own course. Before hostilities began, he labored to collect from the federal government all the arms and ammunition he could get and tried to lure first-rate military men from Virginia into the service of their state.

On the governor's invitation, Colonel Robert E. Lee arrived in Richmond by train on April 22. He had declined command of the United States Army four days before. In civilian dress, business suit and silk hat, Lee called on the governor. Sources conflict as to whether they met in Letcher's office at the mansion or in one at the Capitol. If they met in the office the governor normally used, as is usually implied, then it was at the mansion. Lee would call there a second time, more than a year later, with Stonewall Jackson. On the first visit in April 1861 Letcher offered and Lee accepted the post of major general in command of the army and navy of Virginia. The appointment was confirmed that evening by the state convention and announced the next day in a moving ceremony in the Capitol.

Soon Virginia had two governors. The delegates from the west, opponents of secession, returned home to find their constituents outraged over what had happened in Richmond and disposed to do now what they had discussed for many years, break away into a separate state.

Conventions were held at Wheeling in May and again in June, and the public offices of Virginia were declared vacant. The Wheeling Convention of 1861 elected as governor of Virginia one of the most dedicated Unionists among them, Francis Harrison Pierpont. He was familiar in the business world in Virginia, having been counsel for the Baltimore and Ohio Railroad and a coal and shipping entrepreneur himself. Lincoln readily recognized Governor Pierpont. Remaining in Wheeling until West Virginia's admission as a state in 1863, Pierpont then set up the pro-Union Restored Virginia government in Alexandria, awaiting the day when he would go in triumph to Richmond.

Protected by the Union as Virginia's governor, Pierpont presided throughout the war over the captured parts of the Old Dominion from a brick bank building that still stands on Prince Street in Alexandria. Any Virginia counties that fell under Union control were put immediately under his jurisdiction.

On April 22, 1861, the day Robert E. Lee visited the governor, Alexander H. Stephens, vice-president of the Confederacy, also called in response to Letcher's earlier letter to Jefferson Davis, the Confederate president, expressing the convention's desire to join the Confederacy. On April 24 the convention adopted the Confederate Constitution, and it was approved by the people on May 23. The Confederacy lost no time accepting the convention's offer of Richmond as capital. President Davis arrived in town on May 29, in a railroad station thronged with cheering admirers.

Richmond thus became host to two governments, the state and the Confederacy. The Confederate Congress met in the Capitol, but the governor's mansion was not given over to Jefferson Davis. Honest John stayed in the mansion, man and house outshone many times by the glamour of the White House of the Confederacy, where Davis and his wife, Varina, presided in as close an imitation of Washington ways as could be created. The Davises were not unaware of Governor Letcher's stand against secession.

Governor Letcher, an admirer of Davis, had few dealings with him. The governor spent most of his time in his office at home, assisted by his secretary. He dispatched as many documents as he could to the various departments, where there were clerks—now some of them female—to lighten the load. Letcher's relations with the Convention of 1861 were never easy because of his initial opposition to secession. Now and then the accusation of abolitionism was thrown at him. Turning a deaf ear, he burrowed deeper into his work. In his office at the governor's house, he buried himself in piles of papers.

Hall and porch were always crowded with callers. The need for security for the city had prompted the governor to adopt a system of passes for those entering or leaving town. Passes came mainly from the governor's office until a better system was developed well into the war. Long lines waited at the mansion to have passes written and approved. Some cases called for certain questions, particular records. While abbreviated forms were later devised, at the outset everything was written out arduously in ink, with letterpress copies made by pressing the freshly written page against a thin moistened second sheet. Multiple pages were attached with straight pins, there being as yet no paper clips.

We know very little of life at the mansion during the first years of the Civil War. The Letchers remained close together, receiving a tight group of friends. Letcher had come to Richmond in 1860 in a blaze of Democratic glory, only to end up distrusted by the public. Even though he yielded to the dictates of the people on secession, he hoped war could be avoided. In calling on Virginia for volunteers, Lincoln had asked for three regiments. Governor Letcher wrote bitterly to Simon Cameron, secretary of war: "You have chosen to inaugurate civil war, and having done so we will meet you, in spirit as determined, as the Administration has exhibited towards the South."

Two Union officers, captured trying to set fire to the dry dock at the Gosport Navy Yard in Portsmouth, were taken on the governor's orders to the mansion. The Letchers treated the men like guests, greatly annoying those who wished to make them examples. After arrangements were made for returning the prisoners by train to Washington. Governor Letcher learned that a mob was forming to lynch them at the station. As a precaution he escorted the two in his own carriage through the angry streets, saw them situated on the train, and assigned two guards to accompany them home. Captain John Rodgers and Captain Horatio G. Wright remembered the pleasant, easy hospitality at the mansion, where they played parlor games with the Letcher children.

Thirteen-year-old Sam Houston Letcher longed to fight in the war. Restless in the cloistered existence in the mansion, the boy had seemed so inclined to run away that his parents got him a job on a freighter, shipping out of Baltimore. News of his whereabouts came in slowly, and the Letchers spent weeks fearing that he might be captured, identified, and because of his father, made a prisoner of war. Hardly had Sam returned and those worries been calmed, than little Mary Davidson Letcher, aged three, came down with diphtheria. She lingered for a long time and died in her bedchamber at the mansion. The household remained in mourning for her for the duration of the governor's term.

Heartbreak was now added to Letcher's other burdens. Yet he never shrank. A rare glimpse of him is provided by John Lewis Peyton, a supply agent from North Carolina in need of a pass to leave Richmond by rail. He called at the governor's mansion and found the governor "in an elbow chair by the fireside, among a few chosen friends who were mellowing over their pipes and tankard. A glass of 'mountain dew,' and a whiff of the calumet, put us at once upon the best of terms with the company, and we spent some time amid clouds of smoke, produced by Virginia tobacco, listening to their views on the subject of the war . . . the half military, half political household."

The visitor saw the governor as "plain and uncultivated, and somewhat of 'the rough and ready' style. . . . He was tall and slender, except in the region of the stomach, where he was unduly developed, at the apparent expense of his shanks, which were very spindling—a peculiar configuration of the masculine form, said to result, in the 'tide-water' country of Virginia, from too frequent a use of 'peach and honey.'"

Confederate Virginia emerged as the primary battleground of the war: first Manassas in July 1861, then McClellan's thwarted attempt to capture Richmond from the James River, second Manassas one year after the first battle, Chancellorsville in May 1863, and the bitter winter campaign of 1863 and 1864 near Fredericksburg. The blockade at sea greatly curtailed the comings and goings from Virginia. Governor Letcher repeatedly refused to sponsor an official program of blockade-running, which was practiced in nearly all the other coastal Southern states.

His cool responses to the demands of the Confederate government were criticized with increasing impatience as opposition. Times grew hard as the war bore ever heavier on Virginia. The governor himself was devastated financially. His Washington, D.C., real estate, the basis of his personal wealth, purchased over many years through strict economy, was foreclosed upon and sold at sheriff's sales because Letcher could not pay his taxes in person, as the rule specified. The governor's salary of $5,000 was not small, but it was paid in Confederate money.

Susan Letcher encouraged economy in the kitchen of the mansion. Costs were extremely high, molasses $30 a gallon, apples $25 a bushel, beef $2 a pound, and flour $100 a barrel. Kind friends at home in Lexington sent supplies as often as they could; among these was Mary Anna Jackson, wife of the valiant Stonewall. Salt and meat shortages all fell heavily on life in the capital. The governor tried to sell property he owned in Lexington to raise money to supplement his salary.

Whatever the shortages, and however much the Confederate army might raid the farmers' markets and grocery stores, there were times when the governor had to entertain. One of his guests reported the following: "Governor Letcher received, as usual, on the return of the anniversary that ushered in the year 1862. His guests were welcomed with the broad, good-humored hospitality and dignified courtesy which ever distinguished this gallant son of Virginia. Minus champagne, through the rigid effects of the blockade, the giant punch-bowl was filled with . . . steaming beverage, the smell of roasted apples betrayed the characteristic toddy, and through the crystal cut-glass gleamed the golden hue of the egg-nog, to regale the guests of the Governor."

The food shortage and high costs in Richmond climaxed on April 2, 1863, about a month before Lee's second clash with the Army of the Potomac at Chancellorsville. A group of working-class women entered Capitol Square in a planned protest of food shortages, and particularly the Confederate army's confiscation of food bound to market. Some carried pistols, axes, or clubs. All were angry. The crowd swelled into the hundreds, turned toward the governor's house, and called for Letcher, demanding "bread or blood." The governor's aide told them that the governor was at the Capitol.

Soon enough Letcher stood before perhaps a thousand people. Irritated by his apparent condescension, the mob did no harm on the square but marched to the commercial district for a wild spree of looting wholesale warehouses and grocery stores. Neither the mayor nor Confederate officials could bring calm. Water sprayed from the city's fire engines failed to cool the hotheads, and the guards began loading their rifles, which dispersed enough of the crowd to break it up. There were more than sixty arrests.

In that same month of April 1863 Mary Anna Jackson arrived from Lexington to spend several days at the mansion with her friends, en route to General Jackson's camp near Fredericksburg. She had not seen him for a year, and he had never seen their infant daughter, Julia. The Jacksons enjoyed nine days together before fighting resumed. Then, on May 5, Governor Letcher was informed that the general had been shot. On May 10 Stonewall Jackson died.

Richmond draped its buildings in black and grieved for Jackson, too stunned by his death to react much to the otherwise triumphant war news. Mrs. Jackson, who had returned to her husband when he was wounded, now joined the Letchers at the governor's mansion. The local press speculated that almost the entire population of Richmond waited silently at the railroad depot on May 11 when, amid tolling bells, the train carrying Stonewall's corpse slowly rolled into town.

Valentine Museum
In 1863 Frederick Volck made a
death mask of Thomas Jonathan
("Stonewall") Jackson, a friend
of the Letchers, when his body
lay overnight at the governor's
house before his funeral.

In a formal military procession, with arms reversed, the flag-wrapped coffin was taken to the mansion where it was placed in one of the back parlors and the body embalmed. A death mask was taken in plaster. When the parlors were opened that night, recalled one spectator, "the mourning and stricken daughters of the South congregated from all parts of the Confederacy in Richmond, winded their way to the sacred spot, and covered the star-crossed pall with floral offerings, bedewed with the tears of National grief."

On May 12 a large procession carried the "Metallic" coffin to the Capitol's "Hall of Congress" for a state funeral. Late the next afternoon the body was put aboard the train for Lexington. The Letchers, weeping for Stonewall as well as other Lexington friends lost at Chancellorsville, accompanied Mrs. Jackson.

Honest John Letcher ran for election to the Confederate Congress later in the month and suffered defeat. The Letchers had come back from Lexington to the black-draped mansion certain of a victory at the polls, the reward for their sacrifices for Virginia. Disappointment over the bad news nearly crushed them. It was time to vacate the mansion for the successor, a popular figure from the past, Extra Billy Smith.

The morning of December 28, 1863, dawned sunny and, for winter, warm. Governor Letcher threw open the mansion at noon for a reception. Reported the *Richmond Daily Examiner,* "An immense bowl of apple toddy, besides other equally exhilarating beverages, awaited the guests in the dining hall, and were done full justice to." After drinking and talking for an hour, the company spilled out into the front yard, where they began cheering Letcher, calling on him to speak. Mounting the front steps, he did so with vigor, as did Extra Billy Smith and many others who followed until darkness and a chill had fallen over Capitol Square. The crowd went home feeling good.

For the Letchers a wilderness seemed to lie ahead. Lincoln's Emancipation Proclamation had made its powerful mark. The tide of war was turning. Governor Letcher, nearly bankrupt, faced the dubious task of making ends meet in a wartime economy. Prospects were not very bright for him or Virginia. Yet, for all the bad news and mourning black, a new baby was on the way, and the governor took this as an optimistic sign. Alas, he was to see horrors before the war was over that would outstrip anything he had known thus far. Peace for the amiable Letchers was several years away.

Extra Billy Smith returned on January 1, 1864, in greater splendor than ever before. He was rich, what with the income from his San Francisco real estate alone totaling three times his governor's salary. In almost four years in California he had filled his pockets to brimming. Back home in Warrenton he had reestablished his law practice in a building he named California House and painted his house yellow, in honor of the western gold Extra Billy possessed in abundance.

The adventurous twin sons who had ventured to California were both dead. James Caleb had fought a duel in Sacramento in defense of the Smith honor, and his father was one of five thousand spectators who cheered his win, but he had died in 1856 of unknown causes in the Nicaragua of William Walker, the filibusterer. William Henry had been lost at sea in 1850. After his return to Virginia, Extra Billy Smith had run for Congress and served until he departed in 1861 seeking heroism at war. On persistent application he was awarded a colonelcy in the 49th Virginia Volunteers. Before he had time to have his uniform made he led a mounted charge at first Manassas in a business suit, holding a bright blue umbrella over his head against the hot July sun. Severely wounded at the battle of Sharpsburg, on Antietam Creek, the sixty-five-year-old Smith returned to Warrenton for eight months. Yankee soldiers occupied the house downstairs while he recuperated in supposed secrecy in private rooms above.

In January 1863 Smith went to Richmond to serve in the Confederate Congress, resigning on April 4, 1863, glowing with a promotion to brigadier general, to rejoin his troops and serve in the battle of Gettysburg, becoming the hero he wished to be. Smith learned of his election as governor and his promotion to major general at the same time. On New Year's Day 1864, he was sworn in, wearing a black suit, dress coat, and white Marseilles vest, "set off with gilt buttons." Once merely a popular politician, he was now one of Virginia's foremost citizens.

The Smiths moved to the mansion with their daughter Mary Amelia, now a young lady in her twenties, and youngest son, Bell, a quiet, moody man who served as his father's secretary. Sons Thomas and Frederick were away at war, and Austin, the third son, had died at the battle of Gaines's Mill. Slaves from the household staff at Warrenton were brought to Richmond, including the governor's body servant, George Hunter, who had accompanied him to war and from whom he was inseparable.

Extra Billy Smith was old to be taking on the responsibilities of state at such a difficult time. The war weighed ever more heavily on the South. Public credit was practically gone, and the blockade cut off supplies. In Richmond, morale was perhaps as low as anywhere for, while there had been no attack on the city, as capital it was the principle target. Food was scarce. Some businesses had closed.

The governor took steps to lift the city's spirits. Using his own name as collateral, he borrowed money to purchase supplies in North Carolina. He took a firm hand on the Public Guard and ordered looters and robbers shot on sight. Band concerts were revived on Capitol Square. Society, a bit shabbier for its war years, came to promenade in all its finery two days a week. Peace was confirmed between the governor's mansion and the White House of the Confederacy so quickly that Jefferson Davis held his New Year's reception in honor of the new governor's inauguration.

With a minimum of repairs, some varnishing, and cleaning, Governor Smith had the mansion ready to be put to work. On January 8, 1864, the following advertisement appeared in the *Richmond Daily Dispatch* and other papers:

> The Governor will be pleased to receive the members of the two Governments now in this city, the citizens thereof, and others, this evening, at 8 o'clock, and on each succeeding Friday evening hereafter.

Virginia State Library and Archives

Taken during Extra Billy Smith's second term as governor in 1864–1865, this photograph appeared on a carte de visite sold by Boston merchant Joseph Ward. Now in the collections of the Virginia State Library and Archives, this rare photographic record of the ornamental details provided essential evidence for the 1989 re-creations of the decorated panels and the parapet of the Executive Mansion.

GOV. SMITH'S HOUSE, Richmond, Va.

The punch bowl now, however, held only mild liquids, for the governor, while in California, had changed his mind about drinking. Said one of his guests of a Friday reception at the mansion, the party itself was "First Rate, all we did was to *promenade* and *lemonade*."

The militia officers of Richmond assembled at city hall and with a band playing marched to the mansion in early January 1864 to greet the new governor. "Gov. Smith responded happily," reported the press, "as he always does when called upon, and returned thanks for the courtesy thus shown him." He assured the officers that he had "every confidence in the power of the South to sustain itself against the Federal hordes, and the indomitable will of Virginia to win her freedom at the point of the bayonet."

Victory was not to be. The fighting around Fredericksburg was raging when William Smith took office in 1864, and the Army of Northern Virginia was successfully holding the enemy at bay. In the spring General Ulysses S. Grant took command of the Army of the Potomac and began to make dramatic gains. A Richmond newspaper reported that Grant "had proved . . . that he will fight, if not wisely, certainly earnestly."

He fought both wisely and earnestly, with a power composed of greater numbers and resources than the Confederates could produce. By mid-June he had crossed the James, near enough to Richmond that his guns could be heard in the city. Soon he was on the outskirts of Petersburg, confronting Lee's hasty fortifications. Several thousand turkeys were sent to his troops for Thanksgiving 1864. By then the slow, bloody progress toward Richmond was well underway. It would end in April, when the Confederate capital collapsed before the onslaught.

All around the optimistic Extra Billy Smith was evidence of the dying Confederacy. Richmond filled with fugitives and the wounded. Alarms for supposed attacks were constant, so much so that the press wrote, "Our people have become so accustomed to these marches upon Richmond, and the lesser raids of the enemy, that they are no longer excited by them. . . . The citizen leaves his home, his office, or his shop, in a quiet and orderly manner, as if he were going on a matter of private and not at all exciting business; and the women of Richmond look upon the departing columns of citizen soldiers—the fathers, husbands, brothers, friends—not only resignedly, but cheerfully, proud indeed of the gallantry of those upon whom they lean, in repairing to the point of danger to defend their city."

At the governor's house, Governor Smith dug through hundreds of letters each week, a combination of official papers and citizens' personal requests. In the first months of his term Smith was ably assisted by his son Bell, but Bell died mysteriously in a gun explosion, possibly a suicide, no one ever knew for sure. A succession of male secretaries followed. Callers, received only at certain daytime hours, formed lines that often extended out into the driveway in front of the mansion. When the doors were closed and those waiting told to reappear the next day, the governor and his secretary plowed again into the letters, dispatching some to the departments or the governor's office in the Capitol for clerks to handle. Most seemed to have stayed with Smith for reply.

One day in 1865 Governor Smith heard annoyed voices outside in the entrance hall. The porter was trying to make a caller leave. Smith listened at the door until he heard a female voice, then he appeared out of curiosity, and in his most courtly manner bowed to receive a beautiful woman in faded mourning calico. "I wish to see *my* governor," she said.

"I am *your* governor," Smith said, "What can I do for you?"

"My husband is dead," she said. "I have six children, the oldest not large enough to help me labor. During these years I have cultivated a garden, raised a few fowls, and carted my produce to this city to exchange for necessities of life. Officers have pressed my old horse, soldiers have robbed my coops and garden. I have nothing left and my children are hungry. I have walked seven miles to ask *my* governor what I am to do."

Certainly the state had no recompense to offer. But the governor was affected by the story. He scratched a note to Elizabeth Smith upstairs, asking her to take the woman to the mansion storeroom in the basement and give the caller what she needed. The coachman drove her home in the governor's carriage.

The defenses of Petersburg were nearly gone and Grant's forces would soon sweep toward a weak Richmond. Lee notified Jefferson Davis of the situation in a memorandum, brought to Davis on Sunday morning, April 2, 1865, as he sat in church at Saint Paul's, just outside Capitol Square. The governor's pew was nearby, and Smith saw the president receive the message, rise, and depart, ashen faced. Smith started to follow, but thought better of it and remained through the service. Back in his office he was summoned by Davis. Without telling his wife, who was with two women guests from out of town, Smith hurried to Davis, who told him that Lee had advised the evacuation of the government. Davis had already given the order.

Governor Smith returned to the mansion, where he found Elizabeth Smith with Mary Amelia and two friends. Mrs. Smith took him aside and said, "Smith, I may feel like a woman, but I *can* act like a man. What is the matter?" When he told her, she said, "Take care of your public matters, and I'll make my own arrangements to evacuate the Governor's house, tomorrow morning."

During the course of the afternoon, Smith procured two steamboats and sent orders to the state officials and the officers and students of the Virginia

Military Institute to board them with arms, ammunition, and such boxes of state papers as they were told to load. Meanwhile, in Capitol Square, Confederate and state money and bonds were being buried. At dusk, the governor, his son Thomas, a lieutenant colonel in the Confederate army, and George Hunter embarked on horseback along the towpath of the James River and Kanawha Canal toward Lynchburg.

True to her word, Elizabeth Smith organized her household for the flight from Richmond. Samuel Freeman, superintendant of public buildings, and W. A. Irving packed the silver, tableware, and ornaments owned by the state and transferred them downtown to a vault of the Exchange Bank of Virginia. Mary Amelia Smith withheld only a few pieces, which she thought she and her mother might need. Parlors, bedchambers, and halls were littered with boxes and other paraphernalia of packing, only part of which the women could have hoped to take home with them to Warrenton.

With Confederate forces evacuating Richmond all through the night of April 2 and 3, Elizabeth Smith decided that the best course was to remain in the mansion until morning. At 7:30 A.M., as she prepared to leave, she was told that the city had surrendered and that it would be unsafe for her to try and go into the open country. She and Mary Amelia hurried through a city in flames to the house of a friend. The fire was long in subsiding, although the Union invaders labored under orders to extinguish it. With Richmond blazing around her, a frightened Mrs. Smith asked for protection and was given an escort of Union guards to return to the mansion. By the evening of April 3 it was safe on its hilltop, for throughout the previous night and day men had scrambled about on the shingled roof putting out fires as they started.

The Smith women and their servants remained unharmed in the mansion for two days, until they were ordered to yield it to General Godfrey Weitzel and his staff. Perhaps they watched from the upstairs windows as President Lincoln and his son Tad climbed Governor Street to inspect Capitol Square. Mrs. Smith was shocked to find the mansion's locked closets and cabinets open and looted. Bedding, some china and glassware, and towels were missing. Groceries belonging to the Smiths were all gone, as was the lamp oil and the feed for the horses. Not so long after, a futile inquiry would be made into these losses by the occupying forces.

Elizabeth Smith was given a pass to return to Warrenton. The governor, staying in Danville, learned of Lee's surrender to Grant at Appomattox on April 9. Two days later, after the flight of the Confederate president and cabinet into North Carolina, Smith wrote to General Grant asking whether his state government would be superceded by a military or civilian one. Were the state officials subject to arrest, or might they leave unmolested for Europe? Grant and Lincoln had quite a laugh over this letter from the celebrated Extra Billy Smith. Already the secretary of war had announced a

$25,000 reward for his capture. General Grant responded through General George G. Meade that he had no answers to the governor's questions.

On May 26, 1865, Francis H. Pierpont, his family, and the officials of the Restored government of Virginia, arrived in heavy rains at Rocketts, Richmond's tidewater landing, aboard the steamboat *Diamond*. A large crowd of Richmond Unionists came to cheer from beneath umbrellas. Brass band and cannons accompanied the military parade that took the triumphant Pierpont through the city to the mansion. President Andrew Johnson had appointed him governor on May 9 the day he removed Governor Smith from office and voided all of his orders and the acts of the Virginia

For many years this view taken in early April 1865 by one of Mathew Brady's photographers was thought to be the only photograph of the mansion from the Civil War era. It reveals the design of the front doors and provides a tantalizing view of the parapet, balustrades, and recessed panels.

Governor Pierpont joined a group on the porch of the Executive Mansion during the summer of 1865 for this photograph. Blinds, usually closed against the hot afternoon sun, probably were opened for the photograph. Nannie Pierpont later recalled that while adults lounged on the front porch, children played on the north porch and occasionally allowed an adult to join them.

legislature under the Confederacy. The new governor's daughter Anna, who was seven, remembered years after—in recollections undoubtedly colored by what she heard later—that the parade "was not a very gay procession, for behind the men who welcomed us with cheers, were scowling, defiant faces, and the rain kept falling. The city was dark, gloomy and depressing, and all about, in front, at the side, and behind, were charred ruins."

The mansion, put in some order, was opened for a reception. An exuberant Pierpont, though talkative and animated, seemed, for the streaks of gray in his beard, the tired eyes, older than fifty-one. It was a great moment for him, and his wife, Julia, even more an idealist than he, stood by, close to tears. Known today as the Father of West Virginia, Pierpont was at that moment detested by the former Confederates and perceived largely as a convenience to the politicians who surrounded him. Lincoln, his patron, was dead. In the drawing room of the governor's house he listened to a thousand compliments. He believed his guests when they assured him that a conciliatory spirit characterized the citizens of Virginia.

To the assembled crowd, predominantly male and decidedly military, he spoke warmly of his gratitude and his hopes, promising to devote his "heart and mind . . . to the single object of rearing up to prosperity and happiness, this great State."

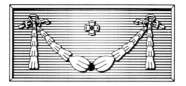

SIX

Gaslit Scenes

THE governor's mansion suffered damage during the war, but mostly from hard use and neglect. It had not fallen to the torch. Most of the contents were intact, complete to the hundreds of potted plants flourishing in the greenhouse. The fire's ravages had been kept from the mansion, the kitchen house, and other outbuildings. As the residence of Governor Pierpont, the compound was heavily guarded at the fences of Capitol Square, at the gates of the yard, and at all outside doors.

Richmonders, their city in ruin, looked in large measure with hatred on the government Pierpont represented. Enfranchized black leaders came forth to represent the people, although the greater part of the population, being former Confederates, could not vote. War's wounds were very deep, nor were they to show signs of healing for many years.

Ten thousand dollars were appropriated by the General Assembly for the repair of the public buildings on Capitol Square. Little can be found describing how the Pierponts spent their part. House inventories mention a few purchases of no particular consequence, some inexpensive but stylish pieces in rattan, a rocking chair or two. Part of the house was kept in summer dress, so the governor could avoid buying new curtains, rugs, and upholstery. Julia Pierpont filled the rooms with potted plants from the greenhouse, massing sometimes as many as fifteen on a single table. "Screens" or "stands" held even more, drawing the eye from tatty furnishings and dimmed wallpapers that had lived through the Civil War.

The Pierponts made the mansion as much a home as they could. Anna—called Nannie—had a younger brother, Willie, and an older brother, Sammie. The children lived relatively normal lives, but were more restricted and guarded than any governors' children in the past. They were not allowed to go alone beyond the mansion's gates. Where Johnny Wise had enjoyed the run of Richmond, the Pierpont children had to stay close to home, unless they went on drives with their mother or accompanied their father to the Capitol. They seldom attended Sunday school and church

David Hunter Strother's self-portrait (left) *shows the writer and illustrator in his uniform as a general in the Union army. Immediately after the war Strother and his wife lived in the mansion with the family of Governor Francis Pierpont* (right), *visible between the columns as he relaxed on the front porch of the mansion with his aides.*

services. Nannie Pierpont recalled pressing her face to Capitol Square's iron fence, longingly watching worshipers enter Saint Paul's.

Having lived in a crowded hotel in Alexandria during the war, the Pierponts found the mansion comparatively luxurious, and delighted in its big yard and trees. For the children it was a paradise, its attic a treasure trove of barrels and boxes of things, of furniture long out of use. On the Grecian-columned side porches on pleasant evenings the children gathered around their father's rocking chair, gazed at fireflies and stars, and listened to him tell stories. He was a fine storyteller, and Nannie never forgot his tales. The porch on the north surveyed a flower garden, thickly planted in shrubbery, with little graveled paths, while on the south the other porch overlooked a steep drop to the service yard with its board fences, chickens, packed earth, and straggling rows of kitchen plants. From the high perspective of the south porch one could see from the kitchen house to the greenhouse, and the long narrow stable building that was entered from two different levels, up and down the hill.

Black servants maintained the establishment. The leader during Pierpont's time was the nurse, Carrie, who had moved from Alexandria with the family. She had been employed just before the war to nurse Willie and his twin, Mary Augusta, who died during the war. The seemingly ever-present Carrie was more than a nurse. She assisted also with the management of the house. The butler's name survives merely as John. He directed most of the household operation, assisted in the dining room by Shepherd and in the kitchen house by a cook, undercook, and laundress. The German gardener reported directly to the governor—the gardener's wife, it was noted by Nannie, "used to knit us the most wonderful lace stockings."

Convicts were brought in from the penitentiary to scrub floors, wash windows, clean the stables, and care for the grounds. Being confined within the yard, the Pierpont children got to know the convicts very well. Called in later years "trusties," the convicts who worked at governors' mansions throughout the United States were honor prisoners. Such a man at the Virginia mansion was Uncle Israel. He had been assigned to the governors for some years, and was perhaps a member of the bucket brigade that kept the mansion from burning during the fall of Richmond. Like most trusties, he was in for a crime of passion. His many kindnesses to the children and his good nature led the governor ultimately to pardon him and send him home to his family.

Valentine Museum

The mansion kitchen (visible below to the right of the Capitol) was the domain of the mansion staff in the nineteenth century but converted to a guesthouse with bedrooms and office space in the twentieth.

Convict Jack presented quite another problem. A friend to the children, he was seen by a guard making his escape. The guard was lifting his rifle, taking aim, when Nannie jumped in his way. He ordered her to move, but in obeying she was slow enough to give Convict Jack the time he needed, and he was gone. Marched to her father's office, Nannie protested, "Convict Jack was a good man. He made my lovely gutta-percha ring with two silver hearts on it. I love him." Apparently Convict Jack was never seen again.

On rainy days Nannie Pierpont hid from her rowdy brothers in the governor's office, where she concealed herself in a corner behind a large chair. It was her favorite room, "a pleasant room," she remembered, "with its open fireplace and big windows that looked out on Capitol Square." She recalled how she enjoyed listening to the conversations of the many visitors of the governor. Former governor Letcher, invited in frequently for his advice, had very cordial relations with Governor Pierpont. Another caller was former governor Wise—now more familiar as General Wise, recently of the Confederate army. He had suffered greatly from the war. His son Jennings, duelist and editor, had died in battle under his command. But Johnny Wise had emerged from the war a hero, while still in his teens.

The procession of delegates, army officers, northerners, and southerners to the office was constant. For weeks and weeks in the winter and spring of 1867 Governor Pierpont and some of his callers debated the fate of Jefferson Davis, who had been brought to Richmond for trial. While most people in the capital favored his release, the Unionists among them generally wanted him tried as a traitor. On the day Davis was set free, May 13, 1867, an angry crowd gathered at the mansion gate. Horace Greeley had called on the governor earlier to urge Pierpont to show Davis mercy. The shouting from outside filled the household with terror, but little Willie Pierpont, too young to be frightened, dangled his doll by a string from the nursery window over the front porch and sang to the mob the war ditty "We'll hang Jeff Davis from a sour apple tree, as we go marching on." For this he was spanked soundly.

Richmond society, which had always graced the parlors of the governor's house, was absent in the postwar time of Pierpont. The Father of West Virginia was an outsider, as much as any carpetbagger, and while for survival's sake Richmond businessmen might appear at his receptions, the ladies always regretted, giving as flimsy excuses as they could devise. Even had they been able to abide the Yankee men, they were well aware that Julia Pierpont, a New Yorker, was the child of hardshell abolitionists and had been an abolitionist herself since girlhood. Although she had lived in Virginia for a long time, she stood for everything they hated. They were more likely to speak kindly about her husband than about her.

The preponderance of men at mansion receptions had become so apparent that it seemed a good idea to offset it by having a social event that ladies would attend. Perhaps with the odd notion that this would break the ice with Richmonders, the Pierponts sent cards to elegant Unionist friends and acquaintances in Baltimore, Washington, Philadelphia, and New York. In large number the ladies began to arrive by train, their baggage packed with dresses, hats, shoes, and gloves of a quality unknown for a while to southerners.

Amid the noise and laughter of a house party of young ladies from Washington, the family and servants worked hard all day preparing for the grand evening reception. Nannie's hair was dressed in stylish "friz." Preparation in the kitchen was conducted with the help of army cooks, and General Alfred H. Terry, the military commander of Virginia, sent an orchestra. Both parlors were emptied of furniture and banked with orange and lemon trees from the greenhouse. Hundreds of potted flowers, forced into bloom, were set on stands, and the gardener checked them hourly to make sure that they remained perfect examples of his skill.

The reception was scheduled early so some of the guests could make the 8:30 train back east. The house party was to remain afterwards with special guests for a light supper in the dining room. It may have been presumptuous to expect a large social function of this kind to run smoothly during Reconstruction. Trouble came soon enough. As the receiving line was about to end, a finely dressed man entered with a young woman on each arm in deep mourning, black dress, black face veil, black jet jewelry. Apparently the women had come "greatly against their wills," for they in no way acknowledged hosts or fellow guests.

They dampened everyone's spirits, but the reception went without other incident, until a young officer happened to brush against one of them. Both women shrank back in scorn, holding their skirts aside, to show contempt for the Yankee. He reddened, embarassed and angered. Addressing their escort, he reached for his sword. The young woman with him intervened: "Don't you see their black dresses?" she said, "They are only heartbroken girls." This ended the dispute, and no other difficulty arose.

The newspaper reports that week greatly offended Julia Pierpont. Few social occasions were mentioned in the news, and in a context of society it was perilous for an editor to mention a lady's name, much less to give personal details about her. The Pierpont reception received full coverage. One woman guest was described as "dressed in crimson, and as an offset to the typical blood of the Southern martyrs wore a white ribbon at her throat." The editors awarded "'belle of the ball' . . . to Miss Grey, of Rochester, New York, who is a millionairess, with half a million in gold, not greenbacks, remember. She was dressed in blue satin, and either she or her prospective pile was the observed of all observers."

Julia Pierpont held no more large receptions, but confined her entertaining to more or less informal "evenings" and dinners at home. One of the

former was held for General Grant late in the afternoon during a visit to Richmond in 1867. The Pierponts were impressed by how little he said, and how much Mrs. Grant said. Particularly surprising to Julia Pierpont was Julia Grant's bold recounting of how she had driven about sightseeing in Boston in a showy open carriage on a Sunday, knowing very well that she would attract large crowds. "I would not have gone," the governor's wife said to her husband after the Grants had departed.

Pierpont's was anything but an easy administration. The burned-out blocks beyond his doorstep in Richmond mirrored the problems of the state. Congress placed the South under martial law in March 1867 and the radical Republicans began passing legislation to punish the unrepentent. Delegates to a constitutional convention that began in December 1867 were divided between radicals, mainly black Virginians and blacks and whites born elsewhere, and thirty-two conservative delegates, mostly young and inexperienced former Confederates. In general the earlier generation of state politicians had been banned in one way or another.

The Constitution of 1869 was created during two years of painful deliberations, with repercussions felt all over the state. Governor Pierpont was not really at the helm of government, for the military presence loomed far larger than his. To former Confederates he was a troublemaking carpetbagger, to the radical Republicans, too soft. His power decreased, until on April 4, 1868, he was removed from office by the military authorities.

On their last day in the mansion the Pierponts gathered in the little parlor across the entrance hall from the office. Sunlight glowed in the fancy painted window shades, and the five Pierponts kept close to the iron stove that protruded from the fireplace. They had often said their morning prayers here during the three years they lived in the mansion. For the last time they repeated their custom, then opened the door to greet friends who had come to say goodbye. To his wife the governor said, "Honestly, Julia, I feel already like a boy out of school."

The first effort of the federal government to reconstruct the South failed both because some Republican politicans resented its weakness and because southerners very often did not cooperate. Being the state hardest hit by the war, Virginia suffered an unhappy Reconstruction. The commonwealth had not been readmitted to the Union. Through Richmond's ruins freed slaves wandered hopelessly expecting jobs from the Union victors. The business community was so stricken by poverty and devastation that its struggle to right itself was a prolonged agony. Tense nerves and low spirits led to conflicts between the former Confederate citizenry and those who now held power. The embattled president Andrew Johnson committed himself to a conciliatory reconstruction inspired by Lincoln's unrealized objective of a hasty reunion. Congress would not finance it adequately. Manpower was lacking. When presidential Reconstruction was thrown aside, Radical Reconstruction—congressional Reconstruction—replaced it, carried out by the military. This was efficient indeed, but bitter and destructive.

Virginia was made Military District Number One, and Henry Horatio Wells was appointed governor. Virginians loathed Wells as the "prince of carpetbaggers." A native of Rochester, New York, Wells had practiced law in Detroit and remained in Virginia after the war to resume his practice. An instrument of the radicals, he was not visible in his role as governor. All evidence suggests that he did not live in the governor's mansion, or even use it as an office.

His successor, Gilbert Carlton Walker, was also a native of New York, a carpetbagger, elected in the first popular election under the new constitution. The circumstances were unusual: he was elected with strong support from black voters, and the election results had to be approved by the military commander General Edward R. S. Canby. Nevertheless, Walker's election carried the promise of conciliation and the joy of a jubilee, and before a large audience of whites and blacks he was sworn in at the governor's house on September 21, 1869. He and his wife, Olive, made it their home. The barbecues, dances, orations, parades, and rallies of the campaign were followed by bonfires, fireworks, and general good feeling after Walker went into office.

As it turned out, he was at first a popular governor. His affection for the Old Dominion seemed sincere. A worldly looking man, he was slim and well made, a sporty dresser who liked white suits, silk handkerchiefs, and gold-headed canes; he oiled his hair and waxed a rakish Louis Napoleon mustachio. On arriving in Richmond, Walker was met at the train and swept along the streets in a parade of thousands to the Exchange Hotel. After that he was much occupied with work. He proved to be less an administrator and leader than he was a public man, and the state suffered some from his ineptness at a time when careful management was needed. Called a Redeemer, for having rescued the state from the radicals, Governor Walker was a middle-of-the-road reconstructionist who wanted the military occupation ended. Even his strictest critics found some things about his performance that merited praise, although riots among citizens and battles in the General Assembly might have been avoided or rendered less devastating had an abler hand been in control. After Virginia reentered the Union on January 26, 1870, Walker did not have to run again for office but was inaugurated as governor for a regular term that ended in 1874.

The record is scant on the lives of the Walkers in the mansion. Governor

Walker was jokingly called "his Majesty." He was said to live in splendor, in the midst of "fuss and feathers," followed about by a "corps of flunkies and pretenders." One of his innovations was to style his secretary an *aide,* while a stable of clerks in the Capitol performed day-to-day under the aide's direction. The mansion was used extensively for politicking, a persuasive Walker seeing that his political guests were treated well. Olive Walker's wealthy parents had always financed the good life for the Walkers.

An inventory made of the governor's mansion at about the time they left suggests a sparse interior from which a good many furnishings had been removed on the main floor. Upstairs the bedrooms seem to have been somewhat the same. The *Richmond Dispatch* described the wood-shingled roof as "very imperfect." It was replaced by a new covering made of tin and put on in this way: the smallish tin squares were soldered together end on end making long strips, which were joined side by side with standing seams. Discarded along with the old roof were the wooden balustrades on the eaves and on the porch. General Canby authorized payment for some new furniture about which nothing is known except the price, $6,900.64.

Perhaps the high living of the Walkers, though funded from home, seemed elevated only in comparison to the poverty seen in Virginia at the time. Whatever the case, it seemed as extravagant as the governor's support for the expensive funding of the state's wartime debts and outraged much of the public. Gilbert and Olive Walker could anticipate no laurels worth retiring upon in the South. After leaving the mansion, the former governor represented Richmond and its business interests during two terms in the House of Representatives before his wife convinced him to move back home to New York.

The end of Reconstruction in 1870 meant the reestablishment of civilian government but not of prosperity. In 1871 the legislature voted to honor at high interest all the state's debts from before and during the war. This terrible burden heaped on Virginia by the Funders came at the sacrifice of progress in education, internal improvements, and, certainly near the bottom of the list, the governor's house. Paying off the debt was a popular idea; even the Readjusters favored payment of the debts at a discount, not their repudiation. During the years when the clash of the Funders and the Readjusters dominated Virginia politics, three governors occupied the mansion quietly until a fourth, Fitzhugh Lee, seemed to pull things back together. The first of the three, James Lawson Kemper, a veteran who had commanded the forces of Richmond at the time of the invasion of 1865, went into office a minor hero.

He was an unhappy man in the mansion. The death of his wife, Belle, four years before was the result of complications from her seventh child-

The broken pieces of a festoon reveal their deterioration before 1885 when the panels were filled with plaster. A tin roof replaced the wooden shingles and the parapet and balustrades were removed after the Civil War, the first of many concessions to maintenance that eventually stripped the Executive Mansion of its distinctive ornament—a process that is being reversed by historically accurate restoration.

birth. Governor Kemper agonized for her, describing himself as a broken man. To ease his sorrow and the physical agony of spasms from a spinal wound he had received at Gettysburg, he drank heavily. Six children went with him to the mansion in 1874. Of their presence in his life he wrote to a friend that year, "You ought just to see me. Although in pain, my children have made me younger and my bosom is full of roses."

Kemper looked and acted old, but he was only fifty when he took office. Powerful with words, he was determined to make a symbolic, morale-building presence. Times being hard, he set off on a path of visible economy. He declined the gift of an elegant carriage and horses. When asked who would be his aide, he rejected any such "New York innovation" and named his favorite son, Meade, as his secretary. When the houseful of children of all ages began to wear on him and his few servants, the widower determined to engage a housekeeper and advertised acccordingly. A stir ensued. In a town of many widows any single man, much less the governor, was fair game, and the principal contenders insisted that his housekeeper be an "ancient woman" or none at all. The right crone never came along, so family members pinch-hit, notably the late Mrs. Kemper's mother, the charming Cremora Cave. A governess was employed, Augusta Daniel, and the governor continued the butler Charles Oliver, a black man who had worked for Governor Walker.

Kemper did his share of entertaining with dinners, breakfasts, and occasional receptions. Now and then he held dances, but his daughters were not allowed to waltz. Beaux were advised to be gone by ten o'clock or Oliver might present them with coat and hat on the dance floor. Most of Kemper's parties were described as informal, maybe somewhat "country," with all the children there and an abundance of sweets on a table in the south end of the double parlor. Even when President and Mrs. Rutherford B. Hayes were in Richmond in the fall of 1877 to open the state fair, the reception held by the governor was simple, with decorations from the greenhouse and little more poured than ice water, perhaps out of deference to the Hayes temperance policy at the White House.

A bill passed the General Assembly for refurnishing the mansion. The thrifty governor spent the appropriation cautiously. He framed engravings of Lee and Stonewall Jackson and ordered necessary repairs on furniture, mirrors, and stoves. Some fresh wallpaper was put up, and some new carpeting was laid down. The woodwork of the entire interior was repainted "top to bottom" except for that in the parlors. Old wallpaper in the entrance hall was varnished so it could be washed more easily the next time it got dirty. Glass-paned front doors replaced the traditional solid ones at about this time.

Kemper probably built the first circular fishpond in front of the house, but all records of the original construction appear to be lost. An established feature of the mansion's landscape by about 1880, the pond has survived as a familiar centerpiece for the circular driveway, and has even been the swimming pool, on occasion, of governors' children and spaniels. Photographs from the Victorian decades show the earliest ornamental fountain added to it, a tiered birdbath made of iron, the water overflowing from a small basin at the top into a larger one below, and at last into the pond. Later in the century it took the form of a heron with wings spread, tossing a stream of water over its head.

When Governor Kemper packed to leave in 1878, he filled a small wagon train with his personal belongings and papers. This was followed by ponies, pet goats, a pack of dogs, and other animal life his family cherished. If Kemper was a war hero, his successor, Frederick William Mackey Holliday, was more so—"the one-armed hero of the valley" had lost his right arm at the battle of Cedar Run. The transfer was very cordial, with Holliday offering the house to Kemper for as long as he wanted it and Kemper glad to leave.

Holliday was joined by Kemper and his children at his inaugural on January 1, 1878. It was one of those nasty days Virginia occasionally produces, with strong winds, icy and raw. Honored guests hovered inside Jefferson's historic Capitol, shivering. Governor Holliday, having buried two wives and his only child, an infant daughter, went to the mansion to live alone. Few details are known of his life there, but, from the outside looking in, it seemed sad. Being single, the governor was not expected to entertain on a regular basis, and even the widows did not call. A year after he took office he came down with pneumonia and for weeks he was expected to die.

Politically a Funder, Holliday disagreed with the rising Readjusters and used his power of veto against them. The abuse he took for this soured him on public life. To worsen matters, hardly had he risen from his pneumonia than his parents died, and in 1881 his friend President James A. Garfield was assassinated. At the last of his administration Holliday was occupying a few rooms as home and office in the mansion, attended by one servant. He turned the key over to William E. Cameron, a Readjuster, with no regret on New Year's Day 1882, never to enter politics again.

The new man in the mansion turned forty in the year he was sworn in and determined not to be reclusive like Holliday or to seem old like Kemper. Cameron was a newspaperman who had become powerful at a young age as editor of the *Petersburg Daily Index* and in the early seventies wrote for the *Richmond Whig* and the *Richmond Enquirer*. His political climb began when he was mayor of Petersburg. In a matter of only a few years he was running for governor in the spirited campaign of 1881. Both candidates seemed equal, until Cameron's campaign manager enlisted the support of President Chester A. Arthur.

With a polish given by his own manner and his supposed Washington connections, Cameron—called "Captain Cameron"—moved to the governor's mansion in January 1882 with his wife, Louisa, and three young children. The public flocked to his receptions. The governor had a wide variety of ideas for the commonwealth's betterment, which turned many of his supporters against him. His proposed free schools for blacks were scorned by his enemies as an effort to "Africanize" Virginia. Nevertheless, by 1882 he was building public schools and hospitals for blacks. He cut property taxes, and through his Readjuster-Republican party the state's finances began to rise significantly for the first time since the 1850s.

The Camerons did little of substance to the mansion beyond repairing plumbing, replacing Brussels carpeting, and some painting. There was little public money to spend. About this time, the ornamented plaques between the first- and second-story windows were removed and their rectangular panels erased with plaster filling. Louisa Cameron and the children returned to Petersburg whenever the governor left on a long trip. He was gone more and more as time went by, clearing the way for management problems in the various departments of the government. He took no interest whatsoever in administration, and even when warned of inefficiency among his appointees he continued to travel, comfortable in a position of importance, seeking out interesting people, such as his old friend from youth, Mark Twain.

For all this, however, when he left office in 1886, Virginia was in more promising circumstances then he had found it four years before. Most of the credit for this probably goes less to Cameron than to his party, for his comrades undertook their work of reform in earnest. In the election of 1885, the Readjuster candidate for governor was John Sargeant Wise, the Johnny Wise whose father had been governor in the fifties. The Democrats, however, through skilled management, revived as a more powerful party than they had been in thirty-five years and won the day.

The Democrats' man, General Fitzhugh Lee, was not in himself a skilled politician. Indeed, the genius of manipulation who had masterminded the campaign was John Warwick Daniel, of Lynchburg, who himself had been beaten by William E. Cameron in the election of 1881. Lee carried with him the nostalgia for the period of the Confederacy, now twenty years gone by. His was the magic of the Lost Cause.

Nephew of Robert E. Lee, Fitzhugh Lee had been a lieutenant colonel in J. E. B. Stuart's 1st Regiment of Virginia Cavalry, which became the cavalry arm of the Army of Northern Virginia. At twenty-seven in 1862, a brigadier general, he commanded five regiments. A dramatic, heroic man, he was bold and eloquent, rough and ready. He had been a popular cadet at West Point but also a notorious cutup, whom his uncle as superintendent had twice recommended for dismissal but nevertheless took delight in him, as did even the most somber Lees. Fitzhugh Lee had fought Comanche on the plains of Kansas and Oklahoma in daring hand-to-hand combat. When the Civil War broke out, he was teaching tactics at West Point. As he left to go home and join the Confederates, cadets lined the road cheering, "Our Fitz! Our Fitz!"

After the war Lee's godmother, Anna Maria Fitzhugh, set him up in pastoral comfort on a large estate in Stafford County called Richland Mills. This rewarded his kind attentions to her from boyhood, and when she died in 1874 she left him a very rich man. For many years he simply enjoyed the pleasures of his plantation and his horses. It was in 1875, when he spoke in Boston at the Bunker Hill centennial celebration, that he emerged from obscurity. The newspapers told nationwide of his beautiful message of reconciliation, and politicians in Virginia began to notice a Lee they had overlooked.

Fitz Lee and his wife, Ellen, moved to the mansion on New Year's Day 1886, he fifty and she thirty-two. The campaign had been a bright pageant. John Sargeant Wise was not of Lee's heroic mold, and Daniel, the promoter, had made this Lee's strong advantage, presenting him in torchlight parades through city and town astride the saddle that had once served Robert E. Lee on Traveller. Cheering, singing, fireworks, tears—all the elements were there, Lee rising to mighty stature in the midst. After such a show, it was announced that Fitz Lee's inauguration would have no military display, no parades. Instead, the governor-elect ordered a simple inaugural followed by the grandest inaugural ball ever held—and for everybody: Democrats, Republicans, even the battle-worn Readjusters came and danced until day.

Lee saw himself as a symbol of reconciliation. While he took an active interest in the state's business, he was a more successful showman than administrator. For appointments, citizens looked to Daniel, not Lee; the governor tried a rather ponderous hand at finance but had to yield to Daniel and other advisors. Virginia tasted wealth during his administration and he took full credit for the new prosperity. The years had turned a tall, well-built outdoorsman into a rotund, jolly man in middle life, who still liked a horseback hunting excursion in the country and a convivial evening in town, but as governor was most comfortable being admired by a crowd.

Above all, he was a family man. The circle at the governor's mansion first included four children, then in 1886 a fifth was born to the Lees in the mansion. They named her Virginia, and Virginia became the darling of the state, attracting admiring crowds when her nurse, in starched white, paraded her in an organdy-draped carriage along the walkways of Capitol Square.

With personal wealth and a desire to be a strong presence in office, the Lees lived handsomely in the mansion. A young and beautiful Ellen Lee

Cook Collection, Valentine Museum

Baby buggies and bicycles commonly filled Capitol Square, which was used as a public park by Richmond citizens and maintained jointly by the commonwealth and the city during the nineteenth century.

On the image frame:

Keystone View Company

Manufacturers Copyright 1907, by Keystone View Co. Made in U.S.A. *Publishers*

Meadville, Pa., St. Louis, Mo., Portland, Ore., New York, N. Y., Toronto Can., London, Eng.

14205—Capitol Square, Showing Washington Monument, Richmond, Va.

A stereopticon view from the mansion of the Capitol and grounds

held weekly receptions in the double parlors. Competition was intense for invitations to her "pink teas" for ladies. The walls were lined with potted palms; vases brimmed with roses and ferns. Long and delightful dinners featured plenty to eat, fine wine to drink, and the verbose good humor of the governor, ever an accomplished host. Lee charmed the entire nation in 1886 with his invitation to the Grand Army of the Republic—sort of an American Legion of its day—to convene in Richmond. Former enemies were graciously received at the mansion and served mint juleps and ham.

There is little record of alteration at the governor's mansion under Lee. At some point, perhaps in his time, it was painted in dark tones in the picturesque manner of the popular Queen Anne style. Electricity was installed in 1889. Light bulbs dangled crazily from the flowery old gas chandeliers, with their sparkling festoons of cut glass. They cast a light glary at the bulb but dim as it spread, yet they were less a fire or health hazard than gas. While clerks at the Capitol petitioned for the return of the gaslight, the new electrical light seems to have suited the occupants of the mansion perfectly.

The administration of Governor Fitzhugh Lee started a new age in Virginia. While the advance of civil rights for blacks suffered an unhappy turn backward, there was welcomed change in nearly every other facet of life in the commonwealth. For the most part the Readjusters, last embodiment of some of the positive ideals of Reconstruction, surrendered to the Democrats, for Lee was the first in an unbroken line of twenty-one Democratic governors that stretched from his election in 1885 to the Republican Linwood Holton's in 1969. With the advent of Lee many disparate elements in Virginia were united under the Democratic banner.

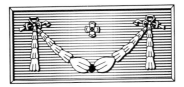

SEVEN

A Landmark Recognized

IN 1888 the Executive Mansion reached its seventy-fifth year of occupancy. This was not marked once in celebration, but was often noted in complaints about its costly maintenance. Many houses in Virginia were older, but none had been so central to Virginia's history as this one. Nearly every governor had lived there since Governor James Barbour first occupied it in 1813. By the nineties the house was being referred to as "old," if not historic. Those who called it home were aware of its long service and in the early twentieth century took an interest in the romance of its history.

The house in the nineties would still have been clearly recognizable to most of the early governors. Inside, the same entrance hall terminated at two doors, each leading to a large parlor. These parlors opened into each other by means of sliding doors and extended the full width of the back of the house. Talk of adding a one-story back porch outside the parlors never came to anything but it would have made the house more comfortable. Few people anywhere enjoyed their porches more than Richmonders.

Governors in the nineties still used the room to the left of the entrance hall as an office. A picture from that time shows it crowded with books and papers, lighted during the day by tall windows with linenlike shades and at night by gas jets and clear electric bulbs. Over Oriental-pattern rugs were placed the desk and comfortable leather chairs were turned toward the elaborate mantel. Wood apparently burned in this fireplace, although most of the fireplaces in the house had been fueled with coal since about 1830. The governor met ordinary appointments not here but at the Capitol, reserving this sanctum for more important sessions. When it came to working alone, his home office was always the preferred place.

The dining room was still in the basement. Probably about 1889 the kitchen was moved from the separate outbuilding to the basement warming room, which was subdivided at one end to provide a narrow pantry. Winston Edmunds, the butler, presided here over cook, undercook, pantry boy, and the chambermaid upstairs. Employed by Governor Lee, he

The richly patterned wallpaper, spittoon, and stacked frames of Governor Charles T. O'Ferrall's office were typical of many houses of the period, but the patriotic and military themes of the art hint at the official purpose of this room. The transitional gas and electric chandelier had an extension cord for the desk lamp.

remained at the mansion for more almost fifty years. Others with gifts like his were tempted by regular work in hotels and Pullman cars, but Edmunds liked his personal associations too much to consider going "commercial."

The parlors of the era were full of odd domestic decorations, all mixed together according to some forgotten Victorian ideas. Heavy window curtains kept out the daylight glare, in favor of the soft yellow of gaslight. The harsher electric light slowly pushed this custom aside. Redecoration usually came in the guise of repairs. When the house was wired, for example, it had to be repapered. Modern wallpapers were selected that did not particularly harmonize with the existing furniture. New upholsteries were introduced in the same way, as were carpets—piecemeal. Families made things homey with swarms of knickknacks, flower vases, sewing boxes, and masses of framed prints or paintings.

The nineties saw a succession of governors enter with mild popularity and leave with none. It was a difficult time. Racial obsessions permeated politics and violence was frequent. Fitzhugh Lee's successor, for example, the highly resourceful Philip Watkins McKinney put into office by the emerging Democratic machine, was especially unsympathetic to blacks and Republicans. He made lurid speeches all over the state, while at the same time promoting the best economic program Virginia had since the Civil War. In 1891 he called on the legislature to segregate blacks and whites on trains and in railroad depots.

Governor Charles Triplett O'Ferrall shared many of those views but hotly opposed lynching and was effective toward purging it from the state. He received the editor of the black newspaper, the *Richmond Planet,* John Mitchell, Jr., at lunch in the governor's mansion with a group of other men. Also in the party was a black member of the Massachusetts General Court, Robert F. Teamoh. Many newspapers condemned the event, although Mitchell wrote a warm account of the luncheon in the *Planet.*

O'Ferrall welcomed thousands of Confederate veterans to the governor's mansion in June and July 1896 for the grandest reunion of Confederates ever held in Virginia. The city was the scene of the reunion, but the climax of days of marching and oration was the reception at the mansion. The O'Ferralls honored Mrs. Jefferson Davis, Mrs. Stonewall Jackson, and Mrs. Fitzhugh Lee. Elaborate decorations and lights ornamented the square. Inside the mansion a band played from the staircase. The three Confederate dowagers were presented by the governor in a receiving line. In single file, the guests moved through the front doors down the hall to shake hands just inside the parlors. After a sip of punch they were urged out through the side doors to make way for the human river that kept flowing into the house.

New Year's Day saw the main reception. It was open to the general public, but it cannot be said that everyone was welcomed or that everyone would have been admitted. The unspoken guest list consisted largely of politicians and middle-class to upper-class Richmonders. If occasionally a hack driver ventured into the line, it might be taken good-naturedly as an accident, but guards prevented such intrusions from going beyond novelty.

Governor J. Hoge Tyler's four essentially noncontroversial years brought the commonwealth into the twentieth century. He was criticized for his racial attitudes—and his laxity on the antilynching laws—but thanks to his support two black battalions commanded by black officers were among those Virginia sent to the Spanish-American War. The nineties ended with calls for a new Virginia constitution. The administration's bequest to the new century was an economic flowering for the commonwealth, matching that of the nation. The Old Dominion entered the year 1900 with good prospects.

Small improvements were made at the mansion by the governors of the

Front parlor

1890s. Governor McKinney repainted the house and rebuilt the greenhouse in iron, giving it also a new steam heating apparatus. Governor O'Ferrall ordered the gas-lighting system in the house overhauled, in spite of the electrical wires that already threaded the place. O'Ferrall enjoyed the convenience of the first telephone in the mansion. Governor Tyler painted the house again, with two coats on the brick, wood, and sandstone trimmings. By the beginning of the new century the house was known officially as the Executive Mansion, but the name in everyday parlance and in the press often remained "governor's mansion," or, less often, the "governor's house," which had supplanted "government house" and "state house" in the 1830s. Governor's mansion is still its common name today.

The first governor in many years to take a strong personal interest in the house and to appreciate its history was Andrew Jackson Montague, who came into office in 1902 and served until 1906. Both he and his wife, Elizabeth, called Betsie, were interested in history. The governor himself had identified somewhat with the national Progressive movement of his time, but he became more regional as his campaign heated up. He was nevertheless a popular reform candidate at the outset, and in his tenure he could count some achievements. The Red Fox of Middlesex left office with little applause.

As a public figure he was not a natural. Quiet and thoughtful, he read prodigiously and talked on a plane that sometimes escaped the average citizen. He shared the Progressive conviction that business was self-seeking and should be regulated; he liked orderly, accountable government and pledged himself to end lynching forever. Betsie Montague was a better public person than he, although at the time politics was not open to women, who could not vote. She had the touch, however, and guided her husband. A story she told on herself reveals much. One morning she went out to borrow a recipe and returned to find a large political delegation waiting for her husband. She went upstairs to the governor, and he descended to meet the callers. When the visitors stayed too long, Mrs. Montague became weary and called crossly down the stairs for the governor to come talk to her. "Just *when* are those gentlemen planning to go home? Are they trying to spend the *night?*"

"I don't know," he answered, "They are talking to me about nominating me for President of the United States."

"Oh," cried Betsie Montague. "They want you to be *President?* Well, dear, I *hope* you invited them for dinner and the night!"

The Montagues and their three children, Gay, Janet, and Latané, moved to the mansion from their home in Richmond and found it "terribly old fashioned." Barny and seedy, it had vast parlors dark in Victorian guise, with

Elizabeth Montague, an imposing figure in her inaugural ball gown in 1902, was a strong advocate for treating the Executive Mansion as a legacy. Her concern brought a new era of interpretation and appreciation, and she fought for a slate roof, hardwood floors, and the acquisition of some antiques.

stuffed armchairs and hoop-back side chairs in great number. Small tables, tufted sofas, and a piano reflected again and again in gilded mirrors hung in tilted fashion to pick up patterns in the carpets. The colors were dark, much later in mode than the furniture, with velvet hangings, lace curtains, and tasseled window shades. Governor Montague made only one significant change at first: he moved his public business entirely out of the house and into the office at the Capitol. In the old mansion office left of the entrance hall, Mrs. Montague created a family sitting room.

The time was right to notice the historic features of a house of state. In the year Governor Montague took office, 1902, Theodore Roosevelt ordered a complete "restoration" of a much-Victorianized White House. He employed Charles McKim, of the famous architectural firm McKim, Mead, and White, of New York. The result, completed in the autumn of 1902, showed an appreciation of the historic White House that, while not a restoration in modern terms, sharpened Americans' already-whetted appetites for the "historic" in houses. While McKim incorporated almost no antiques in the White House interiors, his settings appealed to budding antiquarians Jack and Betsie Montague, who were often guests at the White House, as appropriate for old furnishings.

"There were exactly three pieces of antique furniture in the house," said Mrs. Montague in later years. With her husband's approval, she set out to change that situation. In a Richmond store she bought a gold-framed mirror the shopkeeper claimed was from the mansion. An antique piano turned up, and also a tall case clock, which she placed in the entrance hall between the two doors to the parlors. She hung an old engraving of George Washington over the mantelpiece in the old office. A large mahogany high-post bed, bought for an upstairs guest room, was not long in the house before it became the "Lafayette bed"—the one in which the hero had slept on his visit in 1824. Betsie Montague was still trying to disclaim the legend forty years later.

The Montagues had little money of their own to spend on the mansion but with the help of her husband's friends, Mrs. Montague prepared a request for an appropriation for both repairs and furnishings for the mansion. It was to go to the finance committee, which was notoriously unfriendly to such proposals. Luck intervened. Not long before the committee meeting, a reception at the mansion was attended by a large party of politicians, including the chairman of finance. The chairman, Mrs. Montague remembered, was "quite large." During the evening he sank comfortably into one of the parlor's frail gilt chairs, only to have it yield, dropping him to the floor atop a pile of shattered gilt spindles. Embarrassed, he collected the pieces and was poking them among the fronds of a potted palm when his hostess appeared. She got her appropriation and set to work.

The eldest daughter, Gay, remembered the house as it was when her parents started their colonial revival decorating. "The woodwork was grained," she says, "not in a dark color, but in a light ochre color, looking like light oak." This treatment, although refreshed many times, had first appeared when the house was new, forming a design theme that had prevailed. Mrs. Montague ordered the woodwork's shiny varnished surface distressed to receive ivory-colored paint applied semigloss on all wooden surfaces in the best neocolonial tradition, suggesting not the fresh bright white of colonial times but the mellowed hue white paint took on in the yellowishness of old age.

Intensely patterned wallpapers, gilt-laden and somber, were replaced by colored burlap—yellow in the halls, rose in the double parlors, blue in the little parlor, and Pompeian red in the sitting room—that set off the ivory woodwork and made it glow. Hardwood floors were laid over the old pine that had always been kept covered either with oilcloth, carpeting, or straw matting. The new floors were left partially bare, to frame the Oriental-pattern rugs. Delicate white Adamesque moldings in papier-mâché were applied with glue to some of the ceilings, to give the look of embellished plaster from the period in which the house was built.

The marble mantelpieces in the basement with their arched openings were all removed, taken outside, broken up with sledgehammers, and used to line the driveway's gutter. Colonial revival mantels and mirrors were put in the two parlors (now the ballroom). For the little parlor on the front and the family sitting room across the hall from it, old mantels probably in the house from the start were transferred from bedrooms upstairs. These fine old wooden mantels with their composition decorations are still in place. The Montagues wanted their changes to the building itself to be slight. They loved the old house and wished to enhance it in ways that seemed appropriate to its "antique" character. The governor later wrote of the "quaint and beautiful doorways" of the drawing rooms at the mansion and praised the handsome proportions of its exterior, which he had painted white again.

Life at the Executive Mansion in Governor Montague's time lingered in an aura of a past that was soon to slip away. While signs of change were evident in the Montagues' attitude about the building, the general way of doing things at the mansion in 1906 was not much different from what it had been twenty years before. Perhaps the most immediate symbol of the times gone by was the greenhouse tottering in disrepair, some of the panes of glass broken. Cobwebs curtained the long steps of shelves of dry, empty pots. The mansion was served under contract by a Richmond florist, who supplied on call the necessary potted plants, palms, and even decorative

Valentine Museum

Valentine Museum

Facing page: The Montagues initiated a period of careful maintenance and more deliberate decoration at the mansion. The furniture in their library was eclectic, but from the earlier haphazard office they created a formal and sophisticated room (above) graced with the antique desk purchased by Governor Montague in the first month of his term, clearer organization, and wallpaper that simulated satin. The new front parlor (below) benefited from the Montagues' addition of a parquet floor, Adamesque ornament to the ceiling, and a mixture of upholstered furniture, some retained from earlier administrations but with newer pieces in the Montagues' favorite colonial revival style.

Above: Gay Montague and her pony, Bo Bo, posed in front of the mansion. The Montagues' bentwood rocking chair on the porch supplanted the iron bench used by earlier and later residents. The mounting block visible behind Bo Bo has been cut flush with the brick driveway and walk.

Valentine Museum

Valentine Museum

flags. A pony lot had been fenced in the old vegetable garden behind the house for Gay Montague's pony, Bo Bo, a gift from Henry Fairfax, of Oak Hill in Loudoun County. Here she rode sidesaddle, under the supervision of some employee of the house, but not a trusty: "Their striped uniforms made my pony shy."

The old kitchen house was given over to a servants' quarters, but the laundry, moved to its first floor, was in full operation. Later in the nineteenth century the two stable buildings that had stood side by side at the south end of the kitchen yard were replaced by a two-story structure of brick, with the stables and coach house on both levels, the upper adjacent to the kitchen yard and the lower opening downhill on a narrow graveled driveway. Here lived the coachman James Fleming, a tall, stately black man. Near his quarters some of the convict trusties were housed when they stayed over at the mansion.

Gay Montague, who lived at the mansion from her tenth year until her fourteenth, thought of the mansion and Capitol Square as the best of playgrounds. She knew every employee—"Long Tom Haynes, Mr. Eppes, Mr. Blankenship, they all guarded the Capitol and the mansion, but no guards were ever inside the mansion." Winston Edmunds, the butler, wore a black business suit in the daytime and tails at night. James Fleming's livery consisted of a tan whipcord suit and derby hat, silk waistcoat, and in winter a cape. He wore a dark green Prince Albert coat when he drove a closed carriage. At first the Montagues had a phaeton, a trap, and one saddle horse, besides Bo Bo. Later on, the governor purchased in New York a brougham in which Mrs. Montague made her weekly calls, its glass windows keeping her warm and comfortable on even the worst days. A story is recalled of a convict in Montague's time who was ordered to go to the stable and bathe and change his clothes. In the stable he saw James Fleming's fine whipcord suit, put it on, and departed unnoticed, never to be seen again.

Nanny Green, the children's nurse, replaced Betty, a longtime family employee who met and married James Fleming during the Montague tenure

Above left: The only known photograph that shows the original two doors at the east end of the hallway also records the elaborate decorations for President Theodore Roosevelt's visit in 1905. The front parlor is visible to the right, and glimpses of the back parlors can be caught through the two doors on either side of the clock. Richmond spent $75,000 on decorations for Roosevelt's visit. A parade (below left) downtown wound past thousands of cheering citizens and culminated with a luncheon for four hundred leading businessmen at the city's new Masonic Temple, while Elizabeth Montague entertained Edith Roosevelt at the mansion with an intimate lunch followed by a large reception.

By the late-nineteenth century convicts from the State Penitentiary were a familiar sight in Capitol Square. Convicts first had been assigned to care for the buildings and grounds in the 1840s, and in time their chores came to include the pleasant task of feeding the squirrels. Prisoners, or "trusties," assigned to the mansion often befriended the children of the governors, and many tales of their kindnesses have been told.

at the mansion. After the Montagues left, Fleming took a higher-paying job as porter on a Pullman. Flora, cook for the Montagues for some years, knew to be sensitive to the budget. Money was not plentiful and social demands on the mansion very great, so attention was paid by both the governor and his wife to the costs of the table. Flora's role was not a modest one. Caterers were avoided, Betsie Montague feeling that she could better control the costs of entertaining with her own staff.

When Theodore Roosevelt visited Richmond in 1905, it was necessary for the Montagues to entertain. A guest list of three hundred was composed and this was considered as spare as it could tastefully be. "We can't afford to feed all those people," the governor said to his wife, thinking of the eight-course menus with three to six wines that characterized state dinners at the White House. Plans were made for lunch, instead of dinner: "It'll be the *best*

116

lunch," he said. Flora would make beaten biscuits to go with Smithfield ham, and champagne would be poured generously. "All three are excellent," said Governor Montague.

Theodore Roosevelt sparkled before the adoring crowds in Richmond and at the governor's exclaimed, "Oh, gentlemen, do you know this people and this mansion are ideal. I am captivated with it all. I am tempted to stay here." As the president stood in the entrance hall greeting people, Flora, in the kitchen below, took all the obscurity she could bear and burst up the service stair into the hall, wiping her hands on her apron. With a smile she put forth for a handshake. Roosevelt shook hands icily, making it clear he did not like the intrusion. The press, reporting the incident, overlooked the presidential slight, but the Montagues did not. For Flora's part, she had no regrets but was glad she "took advantage of opportunity."

Life in the governor's mansion is not all ceremonial, yet often the easiest times are those when all one's actions are prescribed, and punctual. Private life is often the most difficult to sustain in such a place. The mansion was not open to the public, although many people were naturally curious to see it. Most days the butler would admit anyone who looked respectable to walk through the parlors, then depart. Politicians brought their families when they were in town on visits. The pungent punch bowl of old was gone; so were the spittoons. There were no crowds of men collected daily in the dining room or hall.

The basement, with its dining room and kitchen, was considered a family area, as was the crowded second floor with its big bedchambers and single bathroom. Someone had partitioned two rooms in the attic that Governor Montague cleaned up for his children's rainy-day playroom. Stored here also were the many textbooks the education-minded governor received from publishers and authors who hoped to have them adopted for the Virginia schools.

Public life required suitable clothes, and this was a strain on the Montague finances. They had to dress well all the time. Gay Montague remembers a dress, "white, fine muslin, striped, and covered with veil lace." She cherished it more than any other dress she ever owned. "All the lace was hand made, the kind people had for babies and children in those days. It was done with fancy handwork, rolled and whipped. There was a broad pink sash." She remembers, too, her inaugural hat. Purchased from the French modiste her mother used in Baltimore, it cost $25, "a million in my father's pocket!" It was beaver, broadbrim with a moiré band and streamers to the hem. When this fine hat fell victim to a teething fox terrier puppy, she had to wear it anyway, and her mother hoped the ribbons would hide the crescent bite taken out of the brim.

Surely one of the grandest events held in the Executive Mansion in the early years of the twentieth century was the children's ball on February 22,

The ballroom

1903. The theme was, of course, the greatest Virginian. Gay Montague's George Washington Ball was prepared with every attention to detail that would have been lavished upon an elegant affair among the adults. Children were invited to wear their eighteenth-century finest, powdered wigs, knee breeches, farthingales. Each "Martha" would bring a "George." But when Flora presented the menu, twelve-year-old Gay Montague and her girl-friends sulked: how terrible the thought of green peas and creamed chicken. They wanted ice cream and cake. "You'll have it," said the governor's wife, "you'll have *all* you want!"

Even though ice cream had always been a favorite at the governor's house, there were not enough freezers to provide for the George Washington Ball. Guards, grooms, convicts, and clerks labored for days at the mansion cranking out the delicacy with borrowed freezers. Ice was brought in by the wagonload. Rumors circulated that uninvited bad boys from town planned to steal the ice cream and ruin the party. The governor ordered four guards stationed by the freezers, which were lined up outside the kitchen door, chilling in the deep snow.

The hour of the ball arrived. Parents filled the little parlor and sitting room as spectators, while the double parlors, cleared of their rugs and festooned with decorations, presented a polished oak floor for the minuets, reels, and figures. Illuminated by candlelight, the youthful Georges and Marthas had a merry fete until it came time for refreshments and a mortified guard, collared by an infuriated Flora, confessed that only one freezer remained—the boys had achieved their objective while the guards were watching the dancers through the window. One freezer of ice cream did not go very far. The next day the stolen freezers were found scattered in the snow on a street not far from the mansion, every ounce of their contents gone. Eighty-four years later the governor's daughter recounted the incident gravely: "It was a *terrible* thing for us. It was the *worst* day of my life!"

The historical endeavors of the Montagues started a general interest in the Executive Mansion that would soon change its interior dramatically. Six weeks after Montague left office in 1906, Governor Claude A. Swanson gained approval from the General Assembly for enlarging the house. Only about eight thousand dollars in cost was anticipated to add and furnish a dining room with basement space below it for a new kitchen. The project turned out to cost more, for the double parlors and entrance hall were redesigned to match the new dining room. Governor Swanson's project amounted to a complete remodeling of the house beyond the entrance hall.

His architect, Duncan Lee, a youthful practitioner of twenty-two, showed a familiarity with both the free classic and colonial revival. The governor's wife, Lizzie, knew Lee from their hometown of Ashland. Lee went into partnership with Marion J. Dimmock, an established architect forty years

These young guests at Gay Montague's party for Washington's Birthday
seem to be enjoying themselves as they posed in the southeast parlor.
Presumably the theft of their ice cream had not yet been discovered.

his senior, former playmate of Johnny Wise, and the son of Captain Charles
Dimmock, who had been in charge of the public buildings before the Civil
War. With an outstanding project and a comfortable, ready-made office
setup, Duncan Lee commenced at the Executive Mansion a distinguished
career specializing in the design of historical revival buildings and, later on,
restorations, serving as an advisor to Williamsburg.

The result of the mansion's remodeling is more or less what one finds on
the main floor of today. Obviously the architect and client were influenced
by Theodore Roosevelt's remodeling of the White House four years before,
but parallel is found less in details than in the tone of the whole. Lee's new
interior design changed the domestic scale of the main-floor rooms to a
more monumental and public character. A principal expression of this was

The addition of the dining room at the mansion in 1906 seemed minor compared to changes at the Capitol during the Montague administration when wings were added to the original rectangular structure.

the combination of the two parlors into one great space, renamed the ballroom, divided only by a double screen of heroic columns. Lee added to the limited ground at the rear of the house an oval dining room, a bit like the Blue Room, only with its long axis parallel to the front of the building. A neo-Georgian mantelpiece with a great broken pediment dominated the dining room and, by its location and scale, broadcast itself to the other state rooms. The oval room was built into an octagonal exterior wall so that useful space was left around the edges for pantries and access to the basement.

Most of the new woodwork was modeled on the old. New neo-Georgian and colonial revival elements were introduced, as in the dining room's pedimented fireplace, the wainscot, and the heavy columns of the ballroom, to achieve the desired grandeur of scale. These additions related always to the original house, if not meekly certainly without a violent clash.

Lee's monumental interiors sprang from the original entrance hall in swelling succesion through a unifying theme of arches that framed a long vista. The old hallway arch was echoed in a second arch that gave into the ballroom, and a third on farther that led into the dining room, all building up to the climactic feature, the great fireplace in the dining room. Lesser mantels with attached mirrors adorned the ballroom, where the mid-nineteenth-century plaster centerpieces and cornices were preserved. Ivory was retained as the primary wood color. Damasklike wallpaper against the ivory woodwork, with broad expanses of polished hardwood floor, gave some of the same effect of Theodore Roosevelt's White House.

Erik Kvalsvik

The bedroom and "Lafayette" bed in which Lafayette never slept

A symmetrical array of rugs and plants draw the visitor's eye toward the dining room, added in 1906 with its Georgian Revival mantle providing a grand focus for the vista. The two new arches were modeled on the original in the foreground, and the oval dining room at the rear of the mansion fit within an octagonal exterior wall that allowed angular spaces for cupboards and storage.

The last major expansion of the Executive Mansion took place two administrations later in 1914. Governor Henry Carter Stuart found the family quarters on the second floor uncomfortably small. Architect Charles K. Bryant was called to the mansion to discuss plans to add bedrooms and bathrooms over the new dining room. Such work necessitated a general rearrangement of the second floor, with practically all the partitions moved to new locations in an effort to relate the addition to the existing bedroom space. New kitchen facilities, a new heating system, and extended plumbing and wiring added up to a project more expensive than the governor had hoped for.

Hearing that remodeling was being considered, Jack Montague, in Congress in 1914, offered his opinion in a letter to Governor Stuart. He felt warmly about the mansion. "I notice in the *Times Dispatch* . . . that a contract will soon be let for remodeling the Executive Mansion or the Governor's House, as originally called. My interest in this undertaking you can readily appreciate, and this interest is quickened by reason of the miserable abortion incident to the last improvements [of 1906], whereby the proportions of the drawing-rooms were utterly destroyed. . . . The new dining room is public, unadapted to appropriate furniture, and generally inconvenient and homely."

He urged a restoration. If space were needed a wing could be extended to the south, into the service yard toward the old outside kitchen. This idea he had laid before "some of the leading architects in the country, all with one accord" had agreed. "If the building is worth anything," he continued, "it is mainly for its historical character, and, therefore, the paramount considera-

Foster

The mansion's new Victrola was recorded by a local photographer in 1912.

125

tion is first the retention of the building itself, and then such additions as may not impair this original structure." Montague's letter was not ignored, but Governor Stuart and Bryant had made their decisions.

When construction was finished, Governor Stuart and his wife Margaret redecorated the main floor and both the "state" and added private quarters above. The state part of the upstairs included the two front bedchambers directly over the little parlor and the library or old governor's office. By removing a wall, a small center room between them, the old nursery, became part of the open hall, entered through a great archway. One of the corner rooms had the great tester bed Mrs. Montague had put there, the "Lafayette" bed. Family quarters were in the back rooms, two existing bedrooms and the new rooms over the dining room.

Governor Stuart was the most private of men, so it is difficult to describe the family quarters in much detail. The rooms were fresh and bright with long curtains of printed linen. Decorations throughout the house, including

Valentine Museum

The two rooms originally built as double parlors defined the rear of the house until Governor Claude Swanson added the dining room in 1906. At that time, the wall between the parlors was removed and the central hall extended through the new addition to create the ballroom.

new rooms in the attic, were fashionably "period" without being "colonial." Wooden cornices ordered by the Stuarts for all the windows downstairs were painted the ivory of the woodwork. In the state rooms heavy velours and Chinese silks in brown, green, and gray damask hung at the windows; the wall coverings varied from grass cloth to painted muslin, with "Louis XVI gray paper" for the ballroom. Some carpentry was ordered on the main floor. The two original staircases of the house were removed and replaced. What had been the main stair at the left rear of the entrance hall and the service stair, tucked away to the right, were redesigned to appear matching. Governor Henry Carter Stuart brought into being more or less the interior we know today.

The attentive care that the mansion received early in this century is recorded in these two photographs. When Etta Mann arrived with her husband in 1910, she wrote that "with all the improvements made by our predecessors it is a most lovely and attractive home and I see little to do save to enjoy it to the fullest extent."

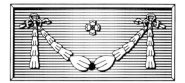

EIGHT

Fire and Survival

THE first decades of the twentieth century saw the ideals of the Progressives dashed by the great world war, and in Virginia the supposed ideals of the Old South institutionalized in the Constitution of 1902. Governor William Hodges Mann, who served from 1910 to 1914 with a stern, moralistic view of his domain, was the last of the Civil War veterans to occupy the Executive Mansion.

Governor Mann looked like a smaller Moses, full of beard, sharp of eye, and resolute of expression. He liked to preach, as well as give orations, and he appeared before black congregations almost as often as white. Etta Donnan Mann, his wife, was his staunchest supporter, sharing his views on everything. She left a memoir in which she set down details of their four years in the "old Mansion," as she always called it affectionately.

Prohibition was not yet law, but Etta Mann welcomed the concept. "I think liquor has done more to wreck the lives and homes of our people than any other evil that I know," she wrote. "It is a terrible curse and I wish it could be forever banished from our fair land." When the mansion's punch bowl fell off a shelf and broke on her first day there, she pronounced it a "happy omen." Leaders of the woman suffrage movement in Virginia asked her to join them and were refused. "I am not an advocate of woman suffrage," she said.

The Manns were entranced by the romance of the Old Dominion, believing it had remained purer than the other southern states. "By far a larger portion of Virginia remained in the hands of the old *noblesse*," wrote Mrs. Mann confidently, "than in less fortunate Southern States. Despite the change the old-time planter had followed his hounds through these years and bravely kept his estate in the family homestead through all vicissitudes." The operations of the mansion were kept by Etta Mann in what she considered the old Virginia tradition. "We adhere to the old ways,'" she wrote. She and the governor treated the mansion as a cherished family home, and endeavored to make it seem that way to all who came to call.

President William Howard Taft enjoyed the Manns' hospitality on November 23, 1910, and the repast was equal to his celebrated appetite.

Around a large silver bowl filled with American beauty roses, the table was set with tall water glasses, each with a little china bird perched on its rim with a place card in its beak. Flowery china and silver pieces shone on starched white damask. Grapefruit, stewed oysters, and hot rolls were followed by waffles, stuffed partridges, barbecued rabbit, and Sally Lunn bread, egg bread, strong coffee, and mineral water. Cigars were passed at the conclusion, mixing tobacco fragrance with that of breakfast.

When the Manns entertained the governors of Connecticut and Rhode Island in 1910, the house was decorated in pink and white, sweet peas massed on the mantelpieces of the ballroom, gladioli wound into the spindles of the staircase, and palms and ferns intermingled with pink lilies in the parlors, and clusters of pink flowers in the dining room. Etta Mann was a frugal housewife, who planned nearly everything herself and carried it out with the assistance of her black servants. For Christmas 1912 she decorated a great tree in the center of the south half of the ballroom, beneath the colorful Tiffany chandelier that had been put there in 1906. In the little parlor, which she called the Blue Room, she received the Woman's Christian Temperance Union in 1913 in the most lavish reception held during the

Cook Collection, Valentine Museum

The bunting draped in preparation for the 1915 reunion of the United Confederate Veterans

Mann tenure. Some two thousand women passed through the hall and parlor and around into the ballroom, to eat cakes and drink punch.

World War I all but obscured the mansion and governorship. Mann's successor, Henry Carter Stuart, whose remodeling of the mansion is discussed in the previous chapter, was the first of two wartime governors. A moderate reformer, he tackled the problems brought by the war with vigor, proudly announcing Virginia as the leader in filling the first draft quota. At the governor's mansion he illustrated the need to conserve food by a strict program of domestic economy, "meatless" and "wheatless" days. Guards appeared at the mansion gates for the first time since Reconstruction, not so much out of fear of the enemy as of caution against lawless elements in Virginia. It was true that like officials everywhere else, those in charge of the mansion suspected the presence of spies, but more significantly the governor had waged a campaign against vice flourishing near the military camps and war plants and was a vigilant opponent of mob action of any kind. Fear of retribution prompted the wartime guard detail at the mansion.

Foster

Twentieth-century governors conducted most of their business at the office in the Capitol shown in this 1919 photograph.

131

Stuart was followed in office by Westmoreland Davis, a businessman idealist, a self-made man, who had returned home to Virginia from Manhattan to enjoy his wealth somewhat on the model of an English gentleman. Davis never intended to enter politics, only to be squire at his elegant Morven Park in Loudoun County. But as the pragmatist in him came forth, he became a successful innovative farmer, and soon, bucking the Democratic machine, he represented the farmers in state government.

Inaugurated in a freezing rainstorm at the height of the world war, Davis might well have recalled himself as a little boy fifty-three years before, in an earlier war, fleeing with his mother from a burning Richmond falling to the Yankees. He served his state proudly, presenting to the public great charm and suavity. One imagines him the most readily awaiting the morning hunt—pink coat, white jodhpurs, riding crop, horse, and dogs—the *beau ideal* of a sort of Virginian who came to be in the early twentieth century. His wife, Marguerite, was well liked, a petite and energetic partner in the governor's projects. She dashed over the streets of Richmond in her Ford roadster, attending this or that war meeting. President of the Woman's Munitions Reserve, she held sewing sessions in the ballroom of the governor's mansion, where ladies drank tea and sewed silk bags to be filled with smokeless gunpowder at the Du Pont war plant outside town. During the influenza epidemic in the autumn of 1918 she risked her own health to work as a nurse's aide.

On Armistice Day 1921, Marshal Ferdinand Foch accepted a "health packet" from children dubbed by the Richmond Times-Dispatch *as the "littlest Blue" in Richmond and a "tiny Red Cross nurse," toured Richmond with Governor Westmoreland Davis (in the top hat), and visited the mansion.*

The mansion was used to entertain soldiers, nurses, and volunteers in every endeavor. From their own pockets the Davises paid orchestras, florists, caterers, and filled probably hundreds of punch bowls—Prohibition having restricted drinking habits at the mansion. The governor was perhaps more successful in wartime than he might have been otherwise. Being at odds with the most powerful men of his party, Davis found that his legislation always had trouble. As he was admired for inspiring his state, so Marguerite Davis became one of the most popular women to live in the mansion. Not only was she seen as a worthy first lady, she was also hailed as a "new woman," doing good deeds on her own outside the home.

On November 11, 1918, late at night, the governor was awakened with a telegram bearing news of the armistice. By 4 A.M. the city was lighted, window and street. Daybreak was welcomed with the ringing of bells, the blowing of whistles and horns. Merrymakers flooded to Capitol Square, and Westmoreland and Marguerite Davis watched them first from the windows of the mansion, then from the front porch, where they received an ovation. When Marshal Ferdinand Foch visited Richmond on the anniversary of that day two years later, a hundred thousand people lined the streets for a glimpse of the great French general. The Davises asked Indians at a Virginia reservation to cook game for the main course of his lunch at the mansion. Their cook did the rest, an "old southern menu" with spoon bread and vegetables in abundance from Morven Park. Dessert was charlotte russe topped with a French flag. Marshal Foch appeared before the crowd in Capitol Square as it chanted his name.

The custom of handing over the keys to the mansion from one governor to another probably began in the twenties. This lighthearted ceremony is only symbolic today, when the mansion is guarded round the clock and a key does not mean much. In the twenties it was otherwise. The square was patrolled, but the governor's mansion was only guarded as one of several buildings. Governors in that time actually carried a front door key in their pockets and upon arriving home late, were likely to unlock the front door themselves. Now and then a governor was locked out, and if no servants were about he took a walk to the guard office at the Capitol to borrow the duplicate.

Governor Davis presented his keys to Elbert Lee Trinkle on February 1, 1922. The two men were friends. Trinkle had pledged to carry out Davis's programs. At forty-five Trinkle was a well-known trial lawyer, a master at public speaking and political timing. Firm in his support of Prohibition, which Davis opposed, Trinkle was backed by the Democratic organization of the late Thomas Staples Martin. With Martin's death in 1919, party leadership began shifting to Harry F. Byrd, and Trinkle's administration is seen in restrospect as a time of transition. The governor's programs were thus at the mercy of a new party organization, which was not entirely friendly.

Dining room

The mansion was in good hands. Trinkle was interested in Virginia's historic buildings and was a principal figure in the preservation of Jefferson's Monticello. He was naturally appreciative of the Executive Mansion. With considerable involvement of his own, he and Helen Trinkle made plans for changes. In July 1922 he ordered the house redecorated, including some architectural work. Thinner spindles made the stairs seem more authentic. The ballroom mantels were replaced by new "colonial" ones of wood with composition ornaments and marble facings "in the same period as the Dining-Room mantel," but the governor complained when he learned (by raking his fingernails over the ornaments) that the decorations on the new mantels were made of plaster and were not hand-carved wood. New plaster centerpieces in the ceiling over the chandeliers also conformed to the Georgian detailing elsewhere. A mural of nursery rhymes was painted on canvas and hung in the center room upstairs, which, although altered architecturally, had continued as the mansion nursery at least since Pierpont was governor.

With such genuine regard for the old house as the Trinkles had, the near-tragedy of the fire of 1926 formed an ironic conclusion to their four years there. In the last month of the administration, on January 4, 1926, the governor's five-year-old son, Billy, held a lighted sparkler too close to the withering Christmas tree in the ballroom, and the tree exploded in flames.

Private collection

If this undated photograph of the Trinkles was taken in 1925, then this Christmas tree is the one that Billy, the younger boy, accidently ignited with a sparkler. The fire spread quickly, destroying parts of the house and temporarily trapping Mrs. Trinkle and Lee upstairs.

The fire spread quickly to the curtains and other flammables and with hardly a moment to save any valuables, the inhabitants of the house had to evacuate. Firemen shot streams of water into the windows as the blaze rose higher, centered for the most part in the rear of the house—the new section added in 1906 and 1914. Helen Trinkle, outside on the driveway, realized that everyone was accounted for but her fifteen-year-old-son, Lee, who had been sleeping upstairs. The firemen warned her not to enter the house, which was by now enveloped in smoke that concealed the raging fire, but she ran toward it anyway. When restrained, she tore away and pushed through the front door, as hundreds of horrified spectators looked on.

Blinded by the smoke, she felt her way up the stairway to the second floor, calling her son's name. When she opened the door to Lee's room, flames

Valentine Museum

Governor Trinkle and his sons, Lee and Billy, inspected the burned-out ballroom. Fire damage was generally limited to the rear of the house, and despite initial newspaper reports about the loss of countless paintings and antiques few irreplaceable articles were destroyed.

poured in after her and she fell forward unconscious on the floor. The boy, awakened by her cries, dragged his mother to the fresh air of an open window, where she revived. Firemen rushed to the back wall of the house, but their ladders were not long enough to reach windows three stories above the ground. People in the crowd covered their faces in fear of what seemed

The fire's proximity to the staircases prevented Mrs. Trinkle and Lee from escaping easily. Their dramatic rescue through the windows above the dining room averted real tragedy.

inevitable, but Lee and his mother jumped to safety. Mrs. Trinkle, suffering burns, was taken to the hospital. The governor's son survived unharmed, a hero.

Damage to the mansion was extensive. The press called for a new house, but except for smoke stains the really ruinous work of the fire was confined to the 1906 and 1914 additions. Ideas for rebuilding or moving elsewhere were not seriously considered. Governor Trinkle met with Mrs. Byrd the day after the fire. Byrd was to be inaugurated in less than a month, and they wanted the mansion restored. This was agreed to, and work began at once. At the time of the inauguration, February 1, 1926, Governor Trinkle had moved to his wife's room at the hospital, and the Byrds were living at the Hotel Jefferson. Billy Trinkle and his nurse were the only people left at the mansion. They occupied the room with the nursery rhyme scenes on its walls.

Governor Byrd made only two notable changes when the burned parts of the house were rebuilt. He removed the large fireplace on the back wall of the dining room. Reasons for this were not architectural, but had to do with the room's function: the oval dining room never had space for a sideboard, and now it did. The Byrds could serve their dinners buffet, making them more informal, requiring fewer servants. Secondly, he modified the arched openings in front of the pair of staircases, making them plainer than before, and they remain that way today. The latter alteration simplified the entrance hall admirably, restoring a touch of its original feeling, but removal of the mantel in the dining room was unfortunate, for it changed the impact of Duncan Lee's long vista through the house and robbed the interior of its most dramatic feature.

In Governor Harry F. Byrd, the state had the head of the party in the Executive Mansion for one of the few times in its history. Often the governors had been elected by parties controlled by someone else. Byrd did not look like a statesman or a party boss. Boyish in appearance, he was tall with a round face, topped by curly brown hair. His high, raspy voice did not sound well on the platform, but he had a masterful grasp of the art of organization. His power lay at the courthouse level in Virginia, where his grassroots network covered the entire state.

His wife, Anne Douglas Byrd, was nicknamed Sittie. She had opposed his running for governor, but took to her part of the job willingly, playing the major role in planning the rebuilding of the back of the mansion. Governor Byrd was only thirty-eight when he took office, one of the youngest Virginia governors, and certainly the youngest in many years. His inaugural address was the first in Virginia broadcast over the radio and also the first over loudspeakers to the crowd. A product of "machine" politics—an adjective he disliked—Byrd nevertheless represented in 1926 a new point of view. At his inaugural he cast aside the traditional top hat and wore a businessman's derby, symbol of the business principles he espoused in government.

He conducted a highly successful reform administration, so effective and apparently painless in operation that the governors of eight southern states came to observe, and many more corresponded with him about his methods. Governor Franklin D. Roosevelt, of New York, traveled to Richmond to see firsthand the good works of Harry Byrd, and he and Eleanor Roosevelt were entertained at the mansion. Guests were otherwise numerous. Winston Churchill, writing his *History of the English-Speaking Peoples,* came to Virginia to walk over the battlefields of the Civil War. He was invited to stay in the mansion along with his secretary and valet. Admiral Cary Grayson, an ardent Virginian and former White House doctor to Woodrow Wilson, was also along and mentioned to the governor that Churchill drank about a quart of brandy a day. Byrd, who meticulously observed Prohibition at the mansion, did not know what to do, but turned at last to his network. He called his friend, the newspaperman John Stewart Bryan: "Stewart" he said, "I am in a terrible fix. I need you to deliver a quart of French brandy to the Mansion every day this week." It was done.

From left: Governor Harry Flood Byrd, Sr., Harry Flood Byrd, Jr., Richard Evelyn Byrd III, Anne Douglas Beverley Byrd, Bradshaw Beverley Byrd, and Westwood Beverley Byrd

Byrd employed an interior decorator, Elsie Cobb Wilson, to coordinate the colors, select fabrics and some furnishings, and advise Mrs. Byrd on the completion of the interior and particularly the state rooms on the main floor. The treatment of the rooms was generally formal, somewhat sparse, to accommodate quasi-public functions. Large glass chandeliers were purchased for all the rooms except the ballroom, where the earlier glass chandeliers, shattered by the fireman's hoses during the fire, were reproduced. Most of the portraits survived the fire suffering only smoke damage, and those were restored. Most were copies of original works hanging in museums or in private houses. The kitchen, wholly modernized by Governor Davis, was entirely rebuilt beneath the dining room. This freed the basement for storage, household offices, and one large room, heretofore used for very little became a den for young Harry Byrd, Jr., just entering his teens.

The house was very full with the Byrds, their four children, and guests. In a search for extra space, Governor and Mrs. Byrd found that the old kitchen building was going largely unused. For most of its history it had served as the kitchen and laundry, with servant's quarters above. These functions had changed to some extent, now that the kitchen had been moved to the house, the laundry partially mechanized with the latest equipment, and most of the servants no longer lived in. From her studio in New York, Elsie Cobb Wilson planned the conversion of the kitchen house into a quaint guesthouse. Dingy, soot-covered wooden trim was scrubbed. Generations of whitewash was scraped from the brick walls, and everything was painted, for cleanliness as much as for color. Block-print linen and cotton fabrics were used throughout. Braided rugs brightened the worn brick floors, and wing chairs, crocks made into lamps, and pine, maple, and poplar antiques of the informal sort imparted a "country colonial" flavor.

Everyone marveled that the mansion had ever functioned without its guesthouse. The reborn kitchen house served, and still serves, many purposes beyond housing guests and overflow from the household. Uses of all kinds make it valuable as an annex to the governor's mansion. For example, Byrd's successor, John Garland Pollard, took the second floor of the building for an office, which he used during his term from 1930 to 1934. Pollard further improved the building with new brick floors, more furniture, and a second bathroom. He ordered the old plastered-over fireplaces opened up for use again, including the one in the kitchen itself, where the food had been first cooked over open fires, and later, on boxlike iron ranges that fit into its cavity. The governor revived the fireplaces for the beauty of their bright fires. Yet, imaginings of past fires flavored the antiquity of the old outbuilding with a glimmer of distant vanished humanity in a way that the mansion, for all its many changes by the thirties, provided only in glimpses.

The ballroom

Winston Edmunds served as the butler at the mansion from Fitzhugh Lee's administration in 1886 until his death in 1933. Edmunds's diplomatic skills were respected by all of the families who knew him at the mansion, and he was remembered as a "thorough gentleman."

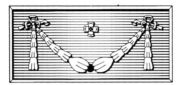

NINE

Old and New

THE house of the governor naturally attracts public interest. Visitors have sought the Virginia mansion out since it was built, and even in early times, when circumstances allowed, they were usually permitted a friendly look inside. But they were not encouraged to linger, because the house was a private residence, not a public building like the Capitol. Before the guided tours of recent years, the butler, if unoccupied, was likely to show people around. Butlers usually have long careers at the mansion, and, having authority over the domestic management, always take a personal delight in the house and its memories.

The best known of these functionaries in the early twentieth century was Winston Edmunds, butler for almost fifty years. His tours toward the end of his service in the 1930s were among the high points of any visit to Capitol Square, and they created a demand for opening the house. Edmunds's vivid imagination stretched his half-century of recollections to a hundred years or more as he told of heroes and belles, mischievous children on perilous stair banisters, and the peculiarities of famous guests. So real was the mansion's distant past to him that he sometimes felt the presence of inhabitants long gone in time. In the upstairs hall the rustle of a taffeta hoopskirt stopped him in his tracks; he turned to see, and there was no one—a lady ghost, he supposed. She came back to haunt him again and again.

Old houses can kindle in a strong imagination believable images of the past. Virginia's governors and their families, in knowing the house day-to-day, gain another sort of feeling for its history that is beyond romantic reverie. They share with their predecessors a kindred effort to preserve private life in the few years they live there. At the same time, over the last fifty years they have grown sensitive to the historic appeal of the house to the public, and have yielded some of the privacy it affords to its use as a museum.

The Williamsburg restoration began during the administration of Governor Harry Byrd. This romantic re-creation of the colonial capital became the foremost symbol of Virginia's past. Restored Williamsburg depicted the town in which Patrick Henry, the first governor of an independent Virginia, was sworn into office and the town left behind when the commonwealth's government, under Thomas Jefferson, had moved to Richmond.

One of the two major reconstructed buildings of Williamsburg was the Governor's Palace, where the state governors had first lived in the abandoned splendor of a long line of colonial governors. Predecessor of the governor's mansion, it was completed in 1933, during the administration of Governor John Garland Pollard, who had been a professor of law at the College of William and Mary, in Williamsburg. Like everyone else who saw the resurrected palace, he was impressed, and he returned to Richmond with a new respect for historic buildings. Pollard studied the mansion's facade, and the Victorian front doors glared at him as wrong to the architecture as a whole. Installed probably in the 1870s, they were of thick glass beveled around the edges and framed in oak, offering a convenient, protected view of the porch and front yard. However, since they clashed architecturally with the historic house, the enlightened governor asked Duncan Lee to design solid doors with panels appropriate to the era of the building and similar to those at the Wickham-Valentine House, the finest survivor among the early houses of Richmond and a contemporary of the mansion. The restored doors signaled a new sensitivity toward the historic governor's mansion.

Reflecting the general interest in Virginia's old houses, tourists began to request admission to the mansion in greater numbers. The first to provide formal tours of the house was Nancy Peery, wife of Governor George Campbell Peery. During the depression a sharpened interest in government brought tourists to the Capitol and mansion. Beginning in 1934, she made the house available by appointment, showing just the rooms of the main floor if they were not in use or being prepared for a party. It seemed a good thing, this healthy public enjoyment of the old house, and the Peerys encouraged visitors.

Mrs. Peery took her enthusiasm to the people. On March 12, 1937, she appeared on a radio show: "Good evening friends of the radio audience," she read from a script she had prepared. Her listeners accompanied her on a room-by-room tour of the main floor and state bedrooms upstairs as she described "Martha Washington's clock," a "French wine press given by Lafayette to Jefferson," a spinet piano, and "gorgeous crystal chandeliers." She told proudly about an old delft blue punch bowl she had found in a storage room, perhaps one of those from which punch had flowed so freely in the mansion in the early nineteenth century. Prohibition was over, but cracks and chips rendered the bowl useful only as an artifact. On the second floor she described a curtained bed of mahogany and told how Lafayette had slept in it when he visited the mansion in 1824.

During a 1932 governors' conference, Governor Franklin Delano Roosevelt, of New York, attended a formal ball with his host John Garland Pollard.

Other governors and their wives would be called upon to tell stories about the mansion and its contents. More and more antiques and reproductions of antiques were carried through the mansion's double doors to stay. Like the Lafayette bed, some were soon blessed with historical credentials of a richness that comes to more humbly placed artifacts only after arduous years of service.

Governor James Hubert Price never liked the mansion, nor did his wife, Lillian. They had a home of their own in Richmond; they kept it "open" and returned there often, sometimes only for an afternoon. Price, an outdoorsman, was a gregarious man, but one who never revealed much about himself. His papers survive, all business, giving few close views of the man.

But for all his discomfort with mansion life he made substantial changes at the house between 1938 and America's entry into World War II in 1941. An inspection of the structure revealed termite damage to wooden flooring, walls, and trim. This was corrected with the introduction of both new wooden braces and steel beams. Some woodwork, including the two stairs, was replaced in the central part of the house. While the walls were open, electrical service was increased and the basement kitchen was remodeled to that streamlined look of clinical efficiency popular in the thirties. Electric dumbwaiters replaced the pulley-and-rope system of 1906.

The dining room did not extend the full width of the back of the house, but left L-shaped spaces at the corners. Not happy eating all his meals in the formality of the oval room, Governor Price built for his breakfast an open porch, located in the southeast L-space and reached from the south end of the dining room through French doors. On this "breakfast balcony" overlooking Governor Street and the side yard Governor Price enjoyed his wild game and savory regional cooking. A new service hall adjoining it linked basement, main, and second floors by means of back stairs. In making the addition—welcomed for the privacy and convenience it afforded—an east window of the south ballroom had to be closed up. A problem of architectural balance presented itself; an ingenious solution was reached. After long deliberation, it was decided to leave the window intact in the ballroom wall by substituting panes of mirror where window glass had been, while on the other side the wall was plastered over, leaving no trace of the window. The mirrored window can still be seen in place today, curtained like any other, but seldom noticed as being blind.

It was said that Jim Price knew ten thousand Virginians by their first names. An active Shriner, he made speeches everywhere and drew crowds. Introduced once to seventy strangers as he mounted a platform, he remembered without notes all seventy when he in turn introduced them to his audience, one after the other. As a politician, however, he fell short of his mark. At odds with party officials and lacking legislative support, he was

Virginia State Library and Archives
Japanese Ambassador Hirosi
Saito was welcomed at the man-
sion in 1935 by a group includ-
ing Governor Peery (front left),
historian and newspaper editor
Douglas Southall Freeman (second row with cigarette), *and*
John Stewart Bryan, president of
the College of William and Mary
(second row, second from left).

unable to realize most of his plans. His contact with Virginia citizens was close both in personal appearances and through letters, which he wrote with meticulous care.

When war broke out in Europe in 1939, Governor Price wrote an inquiring mother: "I hardly think there is any probability of our becoming involved in this war and I would not let this give you a great deal of concern. The chances are that if this country were to become involved, I doubt if your boys would be called." He was soon proved less than a prophet. After Pearl Harbor and the declaration of war in December 1941, Governor and Mrs. Price canceled the annual General Assembly reception at the Executive Mansion. "We have the feeling," they announced, "that this is no time for parties." The legislators agreed.

Immediately following that, and in the same patriotic spirit, Governor-elect Colgate Darden decided that there would be no parade or inaugural ball. A man of few words, Darden gave his inaugural address in twelve minutes and went right to work. The young and energetic governor jogged to his office at the Capitol and jogged home. As an old man he recalled to Guy Fridell his years as wartime governor of Virginia: "I worked a great deal on civil defense, especially in Eastern Virginia, and met at least once a week, in the beginning, with the civil defense leaders of Hampton Roads. German submarines were sinking ships right off Virginia Beach at the entrance of Chesapeake Bay."

Constance du Pont Darden, called by her husband "Connie," was a devoted naturalist, interested from childhood in wildlife and native plants. She kept a "victory garden" in the old kitchen yard, a shaggy lawn where no

Constance Darden, whose husband, Colgate, was governor during World War II, actively participated in many patriotic groups during the war. She was also an avid gardener and took advantage of the kitchen yard to plant a victory garden, aided by her daughter, Irene.

Governor and Mrs. Price accept a tribute of fresh game at the Executive Mansion—an autumn tradition dating to the seventeenth century.

garden had been planted or chickens kept for forty years at least. Convicts worked it under her direction, and the produce of corn, beans, tomatoes, squash, greens, peppers, and potatoes abounded on the mansion's dinner table. Wildflowers mingled with the finer hybrids in borders along the outer perimeters. The Dardens did little to the house. A request for tile for two upstairs bathrooms was denied by federal officials because the materials were restricted in wartime. Constance Darden put Oriental rugs and coffee and cigarette tables in the ballroom and two front parlors. Folding chairs were stacked in the basement to be hauled up for temporary use. She ordered Brussels lace curtains for the state rooms of the main floor, and although the stockpiles of New York's decorating establishments were searched for fourteen pairs, long and of high quality, her interior decorator did not hang the crisp, white hangings until the autumn of 1945. The war was over, and they came directly from Belgium, enhancing a room she considered "Victorian" and suited to long lace curtains.

Governor William Munford Tuck did not fit the recent mold. He harkened somewhat to the mid-nineteenth-century type of Virginia

Governor Colgate Darden and his family waved good-bye to newspapermen as they returned to private life after Governor William Tuck's inauguration.

politician, and found parallel in some of his contemporaries in governor's mansions farther down south. Virginia was ready for such a man after the war, and this one she would cherish long after his time. He took office on January 16, 1946, a product of the Byrd organization, which he served well despite his flamboyant, seemingly independent personality. Newspapermen never tired of describing him; "salty, jovial, paunchy," he had "the comfortable appearance of a man who has just dined on a dozen pork chops." Always good copy, Tuck possessed a quick wit and an ability to poke fun at himself. On the platform he was often a comedian. "I would never denounce the forces of evil," he said of his career, "when I could denounce the flagitious forces of evil and their flugelmen and thimbleriggers."

He put air-conditioning units in the windows of the mansion and glassed-in the Price breakfast balcony but seems to have done little else, perhaps because of the strong dictates of his own thrift. His administration continued the fairly steady program of household improvements that had been started in the thirties. The governor's domestic inclinations were, however, elsewhere. He had a camp in the woods of Halifax County, where he went frequently, sometimes eluding his guards. A man who required solitude now and then, he was as likely as not to slip away from the mansion and walk unnoticed in some Richmond neighborhood, thinking and planning, enjoying peace and quiet.

Being much sought after as a social guest in and out of Virginia, the governor let others do most of his entertaining. Small dinners at the mansion were mingled with Eva Tuck's obligatory teas and receptions. Every official event had the Bill Tuck stamp of incongruity, whether by plan or accident. When Winston Churchill came to dinner, the servant who took his coat and hat was drunk and in the course of outlandish fumbling dropped both. Dismissed, the servant reappeared on bended knees, begging extravagantly for his job. He won it from a forgiving Tuck, who could appreciate good showmanship.

The governor spoke often in public. His popularity was less that of a politician than a celebrity, although his political activities were sometimes very dramatic. When, for example, the Virginia Electric and Power Company's employees threatened to strike, Tuck exclaimed that they would not "cut the lights out in Virginia" and as commander in chief of the commonwealth drafted the employees into military service. So fierce was the reaction that plainclothes guards were assigned to supplement the guard force at the mansion.

Tuck could do erratic things. Once he tested the alertness of the Capitol Police by firing a pistol from the side porch late at night. On warm days he

Virginia State Library and Archives
Colgate Darden and William Tuck en route to Tuck's inauguration

liked to sit on a bench in Capitol Square and feed the squirrels. Tourists who did not recognize him were sometimes roped into long conversations and curious experiences. Two sailors asked the man on the bench where strangers could get a drink. After their conversation, the governor, who had remained anonymous, observed that it was the cocktail hour and invited the astonished sailors into the parlor of the mansion to have drinks with his wife and guests.

Although a heavy man, Tuck was a graceful ballroom dancer with a liking for the big band music of the forties, but his taste for country music was better known. Now and then he took a group of surprised guests from the governor's formal dinner table to the Old Dominion Barn Dance, a famous country and western music show performed regularly at the WRVA radio theater not far from the mansion. Eva Tuck was tolerant but along with Tuck's friends teased him about having hillbilly tastes. "It's not hillbilly music I like," Tuck countered, "it's folk music and sweet old hymns." Country music "makes you forget all of your troubles. It carries you out into the hills among the people who appreciate the real values of life— people who know nothing of sham or pretense."

John Stewart Battle, governor from 1950 to 1954, was the antithesis of Tuck in being quiet and decorous. His work in the Democratic party had made him a national figure and a source of pride to Virginians. The Battle years saw the outbreak of the Korean War and the fear of bombings in the United States. In 1952 the governor witnessed a trial in Nevada of the atomic bomb; back home the rising issue of civil rights came to dominate his administration. Battle and his wife, Janie Lipscombe Battle, carried out painting and patching at the Executive Mansion, and installed central air-conditioning in 1952. His pipe smoke hung in the air of the mansion's parlors, where guests enjoyed their genial host, his fishing stories, and his great calm, in the panics of the era.

Battle's successor, Governor Thomas Bahnson Stanley, entered office in 1954. A wealthy manufacturer from Henry County, he seemed by his gifts at business management and political negotiations the perfect governor for a state just beginning to enjoy postwar prosperity and industrial development. Four months into his term, the Supreme Court of the United States issued its decision ordering the integration of public schools, and the South's political energy galvanized in the issue of race. The governor took a strong segregationist position.

Life in the mansion under the Stanleys was abundant and often touched with glamour. Anne Pocohontas Stanley regretted leaving her five grandchildren at home in Stanleytown. Her children were grown so she and the governor were usually alone in the mansion, with time for the pleasures of

View north from the old kitchen building

Officials in the receiving line at Governor Tuck's inaugural reception included future governors Lindsay Almond (second from left) *and John S. Battle* (third from right), *as well as Tuck and his wife* (far right).

Although Governor and Mrs. Battle moved to the mansion alone, their holidays were filled when their parents, children, and grandchildren came to celebrate.

house and garden, both subjects of mutual interest to them. Their own home in Stanleytown was carefully planned in Tudor style, with broad wooded lawns and boxwood gardens. The Executive Mansion was smaller and not as convenient, but the Stanleys took special pride in it.

The petite Mrs. Stanley loved gardening and fishing, and unable to enjoy the latter in Capitol Square she indulged her green thumb instead. A formal garden was planted in the old kitchen yard, with a fishpond, lawn, and box-bordered parterres filled with flowers. Using some state money, and a good bit of her own, the governor's wife also did some redecorating inside. At first she used furniture from her home, then, piece by piece, replaced it with furnishings either purchased by or given to the state. Having grown up from childhood in the furniture-manufacturing business, she had a natural interest in furnishing houses.

It was a period when official houses and their furnishings were making the news. President Harry S. Truman's renovation of the White House between 1948 and 1952 established a pattern, featuring generic historical reproductions in settings bright with modern colors in paint, rich fabrics, and deep broadloom carpeting. Governors' mansions in other states were

Private collection

Governor and Mrs. Stanley pose with children and grandchildren for a portrait on Christmas Day 1937.

157

undergoing renovations and redecorations, notably in Texas where Governor Allan Shivers was refurnishing the white-columned Greek Revival Texas mansion of 1856 in much the same manner as Truman had decorated the White House. This type of decor—setting a tone of businessman's elegance, well apart from the mysteries of accurate historical treatments—was popular when Anne Stanley began her redecorating in 1954. She was highly enthusiastic about the concept.

Most of the Stanleys' work was completed by the close of 1955. Oriental rugs, damask draperies, white silk lampshades, and woodwork painted in greens and grays, rather than the traditional mansion ivory, completed an orthodox image of high 1950s "period" taste. Mrs. Stanley gave the rooms a personal touch with flower arrangements she created herself. She was expert at creating big, loose bouquets, abundant in blossoms from florist, garden, and even roadside. Roses, lilies, camellias, jonquils, Queen Anne's lace, black-eyed Susans enlivened the mahogany tabletops. While the floral arrangements of her time followed her own style, she also started the custom that continues today of keeping fresh flowers and greenery in the state rooms all the time. Largely because of her initiative, use of the mansion greenhouse was revived.

Elizabeth, queen mother of England, came to the mansion for lunch on November 10, 1954. As she had captivated the nation in 1939 as queen, the queen mother entranced it again this time, and pleased Virginia exceedingly. At the mansion she was presented with miniature furniture, scale models of items from the line of Mrs. Stanley's family manufactory, the Bassett Furniture Company, to give to her grandchildren, Prince Charles and Princess Anne. The governor's grandson, five-year-old Stan Chatham, made the presentation and unhesitatingly complimented her to a reporter, "I guess she speaks English very good just to have been in this country such a short time."

On the political scene, tightening racial tensions alarmed Governor Stanley and his fear increased after the 1954 Supreme Court decision in *Brown* v. *Board of Education of Topeka, Kansas,* directed the integration of public schools. Questions arose about security at the Executive Mansion, and in 1955 Governor Stanley ordered the iron fence in front of the house replaced by a brick wall. Not since Reconstruction had the governor's house been so visibly protected. Threats continued toward his successor Governor James Lindsay Almond, Jr., and Mrs. Almond, touched by the misery of the rain-soaked guards standing exposed night and day, endorsed a plan to build a guardhouse at the gate to the mansion. Completed late in 1961, it is still in use. The small brick structure—initially denounced by arts committees as an outhouse (a "Chick Sale," to be exact) was large enough to hold communications equipment and two officers to monitor people who came and went from the mansion. It has remained in place.

Josephine Minter Almond, a devotee of gardens and houses, inevitably personalized the mansion with some rearrangements. She remodeled the breakfast room with fresh wallpaper and curtains, and added over its flat roof a second-floor study, a little hideaway retreat symbolizing perhaps the dangers in public life that haunted her era. She is more often remembered for the historic silver she brought to the mansion. In the spring of 1958, while visiting South Carolina's white-stuccoed governor's house, she was shown a large silver service, monumental in scale, that had been removed from the decommissioned battleship USS *South Carolina*. Mrs. Almond, fascinated, wondered if the battleship *Virginia* had silver as well. She found that it had been launched half a century earlier, back in Governor Montague's time, by his daughter Gay, who had practiced for days before by smashing bottles against the back wall of the mansion.

Mrs. Almond was especially interested in the service because she envisioned its practical use. One of the governors' great problems of entertaining over the years was an inadequate supply of silver. From the

Governor and Mrs. Almond accepted for the mansion the massive silver service commissioned for the battleship USS Virginia *in 1904. Gentle persuasion and persistence on the part of Mrs. Almond convinced the navy to return the silver to the commonwealth.*

160

beginning the Executive Mansion had accumulated sets of plated silver in some quantity, the sort of silver that might be found in an ordinary house or even a hotel. On a long, white-covered table set for forty for state occasions it seemed small and inconsequential. South Carolina had found an answer in the abandoned ship's silver, and Josephine Almond set out to do the same for Virginia.

She learned that the battleship USS *Virginia*, constructed between 1902 and 1904 by the United States Navy, had been decommissioned in 1922 and sunk at sea in the important mock attack by which Colonel Billy Mitchell demonstrated to military brass the strategic advantages of airplanes. Further research revealed that the ship's silver, commissioned by the General Assembly in 1906 and paid for by the commonwealth, had been transferred first to the USS *Richmond* and then to the USS *Roanoke* in the Pacific. Mrs. Almond was delighted to find that the *Roanoke* had recently been decommissioned and the silver crated for temporary storage in a warehouse in San

Dismayed by the plight of the guards in heat, snow, and rain, Mrs. Almond asked that a small shelter be built for them at the mansion's gate.

Francisco. But getting it proved difficult, for others had asked first. The navy had promised it to the officers' club at Quantico. Governor Almond made some telephone calls; inquiry rose to warm dialogue, with a resolute lady in the wings, and at last the navy reluctantly returned the silver to Virginia. After a brief delay on the mansion driveway, where the governor had to produce $165 in collect shipping costs, Josephine Almond spread the silver lovingly over the long banquet table in the mansion. The heavy service, still the pride of the house, consists of fifty pieces, which Mrs. Almond arranged in glass-front cases she ordered built into the walls of the stair halls. She could not stand the thought of hiding it away in Pacific cloth between uses. Magnificent in scale, the heavy silver service is engaging in the innocent, almost folk-art character of its design. It was crafted in the era of the three-hundredth anniversary of Jamestown. Each of the fifty pieces is thus richly worked in decorations inspired by Virginia history, from cups to serving dishes, plates, and bowls. The heroic eight-gallon punch bowl is etched with a view of the Capitol and medallion portraits of the then seven Virginia-born presidents of the United States (Woodrow Wilson, president after the silver was made, was the eighth). On the great tray is an etched scene representing the Jamestown landing, with Indians and Englishmen and the shoreline as it might have looked in 1607.

Industrial prosperity spawned by World War II continued in peacetime in a more general economic improvement in Virginia. Through the intervening forty years the pace of growth has increased, bringing with it a great variety of endeavor, and in the 1980s a state economy relatively stable through diversification. With sharp changes usually comes a search for a past to support the altered identity. As part of the revived interest in Virginia history the governor's house received more attention than ever before.

Governor Albertis Sydney Harrison, Jr., and his wife, Lacey Virginia Harrison, produced in a limited edition at Christmas in 1965 a trim twenty-page booklet about the Executive Mansion, with color photographs of the state rooms. Although limited in circulation, the booklet promoted the mansion as a significant historic site, and its influence on future perspectives on the house was considerable. Public curiosity about the mansion was a new reason for opening it for public inspection.

Meanwhile, a revival of historic houses had been already flourishing elsewhere. In France, during the presidency of Charles de Gaulle, important seventeenth- and eighteenth-century palaces were undergoing restoration in the late 1950s and early 1960s. President and Mrs. John F. Kennedy were captivated by the restoration idea on a state visit to France, four months after his inauguration in 1961, when received by de Gaulle in a room at Versailles specially furnished with French objects related to American history. Not long after, the Kennedys announced plans to refurnish the White House in antiques, dubbing it a "restoration." The nation admired the youthful first lady who created with decorative arts a colorful and lustrous aura of American history. State governors watched with interest, too, and in the ensuing years nearly all the states with historic or architecturally distinguished official residences in one way or another came to mirror the Kennedy White House.

In the most effective of these restorations the design plans took their themes from the history of the houses themselves. If in France the memory of Marie Antoinette hovered over de Gaulle's Versailles, and Jefferson was an assumed presence in the Kennedy Green Room, then it followed that the ghost of Extra Billy would demand deference at Virginia's Executive Mansion, the oldest of all the governors' residences still in use. Paradoxically, in this case, history and romance were not to play much of a part.

The idea of a historical redecoration of the Executive Mansion made its formal appearance with Linwood Holton in 1970, the first Republican governor of Virginia since the 1880s. The governor and his wife, Virginia Rogers Holton, serving under the newly revised state constitution and eager to dramatize a new era, decided that the mansion might better express the long history that made it outstanding among state governors' houses. On January 12, 1973, Governor Holton assembled interested parties at the mansion and announced his plans to send legislation to the General Assembly creating an advisory committee to oversee "a thorough research program designed to develop a better understanding and awareness of the history and significance of the Executive Mansion." No money was sought from the assembly, only its blessing and a legally constituted framework for private fund-raising by a committee initially composed, for the most part, of the citizens brought together at the mansion that day. Everyone involved felt good about the project, and was eager to set to work. The spirit was contagious. Woody Holton, aged thirteen, got ahead of the game by setting up a concession outside: "Tours of the Mansion—75 cents."

After the bill became law, the Citizens Advisory Council for Interpreting and Furnishing the Executive Mansion turned for advice to the most obvious sources at hand, the Colonial Williamsburg Foundation and the White House, which was then undergoing a new program of antiques collecting during the administration of the Republican Richard M. Nixon. Richmond historian Connie H. Wyrick prepared a historical study about the mansion's furnishings that was originally meant to form the basis of planning for the interior decoration of the rooms. The collecting of furnishings, however, moved on faster than the research. Time constraints inevitable in such public houses altered the original objective to a generic treatment based upon historical period decor, the philosophy espoused in museums of furniture and decorative arts. A stringent definition of

Private collection

Above, from left: Linwood Holton III, Virginia Tayloe Holton, Governor A. Linwood Holton, Jr., Dwight Holton, Virginia Rogers Holton, and Anne Bright Holton.

Left: Governor and Mrs. Albertis S. Harrison, Jr.

Private collection Norfolk Virginian-Pilot

Left: Governor and Mrs. Mills E. Godwin, Jr., pose with their daughter, Becky, during Governor Godwin's first administration. Right: Mrs. Godwin and Tom Bannister, head butler for many years, decorated the mansion Christmas tree in 1966.

appropriateness was presented to the committee restricting acceptable furnishings to American objects of the eighteenth and early-nineteenth centuries. The work of redecorating was to be carried out one room at a time. Furnishings were acquired in impressive number throughout the Holton administration and into that of his three immediate successors, Mills E. Godwin, Jr., John N. Dalton, and Charles S. Robb.

Gifts of antiques and donations of money made it possible to assemble for the public rooms a profusion of wing chairs, sofas, gilt mirrors, and small tables in mahogany. Governor and Mrs. Mills E. Godwin, Jr., gave their support to the program. During the second Godwin administration Katherine Godwin yielded her own earlier ballroom color scheme of cream and gold to a new one the committee selected, light blue and beige, and thus encouraged the committee to assume responsibility for decisions about the interior. Commissioned by the Virginia Chamber of Commerce to write a much-needed guide to the house, she produced a charming personal account, *Living in a Legacy* (1977), which though long out of print today, in

its time was distributed widely and generated interest in the mansion life and traditions.

Still the committee's main effort was in buying furnishings. The pilot project, the little parlor, was officially opened at a reception on May 30, 1975, a prim Yankee interior arranged with delicate Federal furnishings. It was a contrast in scale to the heavier New England colonial pieces donated for the former office across the hall.

As the collection developed, artwork was also acquired by gift, purchase, and loan, and in this a concentration on Virginia subject matter gave the rooms a significance of place. To the existing group of random Virginia portraits were added views and scenes around the state, most of them nineteenth-century paintings in oil. Some fine historical portraits were acquired during the administration of Governor Dalton, notably that of Governor Henry A. Wise as a young man. The collection extended to include portraits of celebrated Virginians, as for example, Peter Francisco, revolutionary war luminary and longtime sergeant at arms of the General Assembly. A physical giant, the amiable Francisco fills his gilt frame. The fastidious governor who first occupied the house, James Barbour, also looks down from the wall.

Richmond Newspapers
Posing in the ballroom before the inaugural ball of Governor John N. Dalton were (left to right) *John N. Dalton, Jr., Governor Dalton, Ted W. Dalton, Mary Helen Dalton, Eddy Dalton, and Katherine Dalton.*

Governor John N. Dalton, pledging a "New Dominion," continued the Republican reign in the Executive Mansion. In the bitter January of 1978 he entered the house the Godwins had left brimming with red poinsettias. If one room is best remembered for the Dalton tenure it is the dining room, where their acclaimed menus were assembled in a book, *Dining With the Daltons*, by the governor's wife, Eddy Dalton. Proceeds from the book went to the First Lady's Mental Retardation Project, which Eddy Dalton sponsored. The collecting of antiques continued vigorously under Dalton, and, by the Democrats' return with Charles S. Robb, the state rooms had been redecorated, so the program slowed down.

Charles and Lynda Robb completely renovated and modernized the family quarters. An interest in history led them to open the house for regular tours four days a week. Few changes were made in the historic parts of the house, but the Victorian fountain in front was restored to its simpler early

The kitchen beneath the dining room

Above left: Governor and Mrs. Charles S. Robb posed behind the cake at a party for their fifteenth wedding anniversary. Above right: Governor Gerald L. Baliles, Laura Baliles, Jonathan Baliles, and Jeannie P. Baliles in the upstairs sitting room at the Executive Mansion. Below, from the left: First Ladies Godwin, Harrison, Darden, Robb, Almond, Dalton, and Holton at a reunion in the Executive Mansion.

form, and the exotic iron bird—well worn by the elements—sent to honorable retirement in storage.

As the one-hundred-seventy-fifth anniversary of the mansion approached in the mid-1980s, the committee revived the original idea of historical scholarship, branching both into the publication of a history book and some restoration to the mansion. Unique among committees of its kind for its large size and careful mix in membership of public officials, private

Erik Kvalsvik

A gift to Governor and Mrs. Baliles, this doghouse stands near the old kitchen. Partially visible behind the doghouse is the inscription on the base of a small statue, Joy of Life, *given to Mrs. John Garland Pollard by sculptor Attilio Piccirilli and placed near the old kitchen "in accordance with her wish . . . among the trees and shrubs she planted."*

citizens, and professional scholars, the Citizens Advisory Council's first act of restoration was during the Gerald L. Baliles administration, to reconstruct the wooden roof balustrades and the ornamented panels on the outside walls complete with their stuccoed garlands.

A hundred years ago Governor Fitzhugh Lee's children took a diamond and cut their initials into a mansion windowpane. This glass pane survives, an odd and unique commemoration of one family's tenure. Few physical traces—odd or not—remain of the passing gubernatorial generations. Busy with the present, the house holds on to very few bits and pieces of its own movable past. Household things wear out and are replaced. Even the oldest of the furnishings now in use rarely have been in the house for more than, say, fifty years. Most were brought in within the last two decades, with no previous mansion provenance. But the interiors are not untouchable reliquaries, and in an ongoing house this is as it must be.

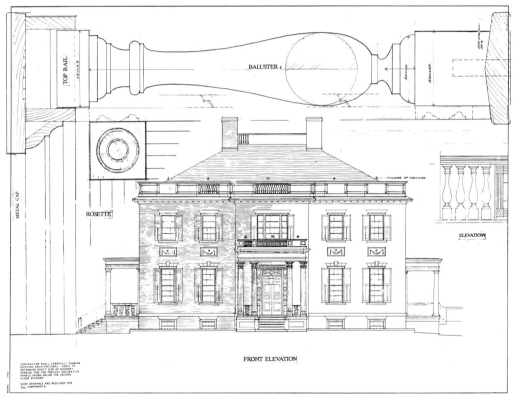

Henry J. Browne

This elevation by Henry Browne, of Charlottesville, shows the mansion as it will appear after the restoration of the decorative panels between the windows, the balustrade above the front porch, and the parapet above the eaves—a project scheduled for completion in 1989.

Considered at first glance today, the Executive Mansion does not seem especially old. Its brick walls are freshly painted. Clipped lawn rolls up against the brick driveway, and the fountain splashes into its second century as fresh as though it were first turned on moments ago. The building is nevertheless an enduring chronicle: the original house survives in large measure, and for this century we see Governor Swanson's ballroom of 1906; one still enters through Governor Pollard's authentic front doors—or doors just like them; the upstairs sanctum built by Mrs. Almond is still a favorite mansion retreat; and the gardens, an accumulation of the horticultural fascinations of a half-century's governors and governors' wives, bloom dependably in spring and in fervent summer envelop the house in shades of cool green.

Taylor Dabney

Since 1830, all of Virginia's constitutions have rendered governors ineligible to succeed themselves. Mills E. Godwin, Jr., the only twentieth-century governor to serve two terms, is pictured here with Governors Linwood Holton, Jr., Gerald L. Baliles, Lindsay Almond, Jr., and Charles S. Robb at a party at the Executive Mansion in 1988.

Artist Vernon P. Johnson's conception of the restored mansion

The mementos of everyday life, however, slip away. Families serve their years at the mansion and depart, taking their own belongings, leaving for their successors those objects bought by or donated to the state. This pattern has continued for all the years the house has sheltered the governors. Experiences of life, in contrast, linger in spoken legend. The activities of many people accumulating over time have become the shared memory of the mansion, a treasure of human anecdote and emotion of almost incomprehensible extent.

Because the house serves every day without deference to its age, it is often repaired, and altered in small ways. Change is neither unusual nor are sensible changes necessarily unfortunate in official houses. The mansion may share Capitol Square with the bronze and granite monuments visible from its porch, but, while it is inescapably a monument as well, its character is not the same. A long passage of years and people has not turned it into a symbol of the office of governor, but have deeply entrenched it in the popular mind as a home. The meaning it gives us is reassuringly simple: here is the house where the governor lives, and where nearly all of the governors have lived in the past. At once old and new, its glory is its constant presence in the path of Virginia history.

Appendix A
Governors of the Commonwealth of Virginia

FROM 1776 to 1852 the governor was chosen by the legislature and, if the office became vacant by death or resignation, the president or senior member of the Council of State acted as governor until the assembly chose a successor. Since 1852 the governor has been elected by popular vote, except during Reconstruction, 1865-1869, when provisional governors were named by federal authorities. SOURCE: Emily J. Salmon, ed., *A Hornbook of Virginia History*, 3d ed. (Richmond: Virginia State Library, 1983), 76-81.

Patrick Henry, July 6, 1776–June 1, 1779.

Thomas Jefferson, June 2, 1779–June 3, 1781.

William Fleming, member of the Council of State acting as governor, June 4-12, 1781.

Thomas Nelson, Jr., June 12–November 22, 1781.

David Jameson, member of the Council of State acting as governor, November 22-30, 1781.

Benjamin Harrison, December 1, 1781–November 30, 1784.

Patrick Henry, November 30, 1784–November 30, 1786.

Edmund Randolph, November 30, 1786–November 12, 1788.

Beverley Randolph, November 12, 1788–December 1, 1791.

Henry Lee, December 1, 1791–December 1, 1794.

Robert Brooke, December 1, 1794–November 30, 1796.

James Wood, November 30, 1796–December 6, 1799.

Hardin Burnley, member of the Council of State acting as governor, December 7-11, 1799.

John Pendleton, member of the Council of State acting as governor, December 11-19, 1799.

James Monroe, December 19, 1799–December 24, 1802.

John Page, December 24, 1802–December 11, 1805.

William H. Cabell, December 11, 1805–December 12, 1808.

John Tyler, Sr., December 12, 1808–January 15, 1811.

George William Smith, member of the Council of State acting as governor, January 15-19, 1811.

James Monroe, January 19–April 3, 1811.

George William Smith, member of the Council of State acting as governor, April 3–December 6, 1811; governor, December 6-26, 1811.

Peyton Randolph, member of Council of State acting as governor, December 27, 1811–January 4, 1812.

James Barbour, January 4, 1812–December 11, 1814.

Wilson Cary Nicholas, December 11, 1814–December 11, 1816.

James Patton Preston, December 11, 1816–December 11, 1819.

Thomas Mann Randolph, December 11, 1819–December 11, 1822.

James Pleasants, December 11, 1822–December 11, 1825.

John Tyler, Jr., December 11, 1825–March 4, 1827.

William Branch Giles, March 4, 1827–March 4, 1830.

John Floyd, March 4, 1830–March 31, 1834.

Littleton Waller Tazewell, March 31, 1834–March 30, 1836.

Wyndham Robertson, member of the Council of State acting as governor, March 30, 1836–March 31, 1837.

David Campbell, March 31, 1837–March 31, 1840.

Thomas Walker Gilmer, March 31, 1840–March 20, 1841.

John Mercer Patton, member of the Council of State acting as governor, March 20–31, 1841.

John Rutherfoord, member of the Council of State acting as governor, March 31, 1841–March 31, 1842.

John Munford Gregory, member of the Council of State acting as governor, March 31, 1842–January 5, 1843.

James McDowell, January 5, 1843–January 1, 1846.

William Smith, January 1, 1846–January 1, 1849.

John Buchanan Floyd, January 1, 1849–January 1, 1852.

Joseph Johnson, January 1, 1852–January 1, 1856.

Henry Alexander Wise, January 1, 1856–January 1, 1860.

John Letcher, January 1, 1860–January 1, 1864.

William Smith, January 1, 1864–May 9, 1865; Smith did not formally surrender his office until May 20.

Francis Harrison Pierpont, governor of the Restored government at Wheeling, June 20, 1861–August 28, 1863, and Alexandria, August 28, 1863–May 9, 1865.

Francis Harrison Pierpont, provisional governor, May 9, 1865–April 4, 1868.

Henry Horatio Wells, provisional governor, April 4, 1868–September 21, 1869.

Gilbert Carlton Walker, provisional governor, September 21–December 31, 1869; governor, January 1, 1870–January 1, 1874.

James Lawson Kemper, January 1, 1874–January 1, 1878.

Frederick William Mackey Holliday, January 1, 1878–January 1, 1882.

William Evelyn Cameron, January 1, 1882–January 1, 1886.

Fitzhugh Lee, January 1, 1886–January 1, 1890.

Philip Watkins McKinney, January 1, 1890–January 1, 1894.

Charles Triplett O'Ferrall, January 1, 1894–January 1, 1898.

James Hoge Tyler, January 1, 1898–January 1, 1902.

Andrew Jackson Montague, January 1, 1902–February 1, 1906.

Claude Augustus Swanson, February 1, 1906–February 1, 1910.

William Hodges Mann, February 1, 1910–February 1, 1914.

Henry Carter Stuart, February 1, 1914–February 1, 1918.

Westmoreland Davis, February 1, 1918–February 1, 1922.

Elbert Lee Trinkle, February 1, 1922–February 1, 1926.

Harry Flood Byrd, Sr., February 1, 1926–January 15, 1930.

John Garland Pollard, January 15, 1930–January 16, 1934.

George Campbell Peery, January 17, 1934–January 18, 1938.

James Hubert Price, January 19, 1938–January 20, 1942.

Colgate Whitehead Darden, Jr., January 21, 1942–January 15, 1946.

William Munford Tuck, January 16, 1946–January 17, 1950.

John Stewart Battle, January 18, 1950–January 19, 1954.

Thomas Bahnson Stanley, January 20, 1954–January 11, 1958.

James Lindsay Almond, Jr., January 11, 1958–January 13, 1962.

Albertis Sydney Harrison, Jr., January 13, 1962–January 15, 1966.
Mills Edwin Godwin, Jr., January 15, 1966–January 17, 1970.
Abner Linwood Holton, Jr., January 17, 1970–January 12, 1974.
Mills Edwin Godwin, Jr., January 12, 1974–January 14, 1978.
John Nichols Dalton, January 14, 1978–January 16, 1982.
Charles Spittal Robb, January 16, 1982–January 11, 1986.
Gerald Lee Baliles, January 11, 1986–

Appendix B
Selected Documents, 1811–1813

Document 1. An Act directing the Sale of
certain Public Property, and for other purposes.
[Passed February 13, 1811.]

1. *Be it enacted by the General Assembly,* That Matthew Cheatham, Nathaniel Selden, David Bullock, William M'Kim, Abraham B. Venable, William Wirt and Robert Greenhow, be, and are hereby appointed commissioners, who, or a majority of whom, shall have power to contract for the building of a house for the use of the governor of the commonwealth, on the lot on which the present governor's house stands.

2. *Be it further enacted,* That for the erection and completion of said building, the sum of twelve thousand dollars shall be appropriated, which sum the said commissioners shall not have power to exceed; nor shall the commonwealth in case of excess be in any wise liable therefor. The commissioners aforesaid shall also have power to sell at public auction, for cash, or on a short credit, the lot of ground lying between Wright Southgate's and Edmund Randolph's, and to convey to the purchaser or purchasers, all the commonwealth's title to, and interest in said lot; and also to sell for the best price that can be obtained, the materials of which the present governor's house is composed, and the monies arising from such sales it shall be their duty to pay into the public treasury.

3. *Be it further enacted,* That for the present accommodation of the governor, the commissioners aforesaid are hereby authorised to rent, for one year, on the best terms, a suitable and convenient house in the city of Richmond.

4. This act shall commence and be in force from and after the passing thereof.

Document 2. An Act to provide a Temporary Residence
for the Governor or Chief Magistrate of this Commonwealth,
and for other purposes. [Passed January 16, 1812.]

1. *Be it enacted by the General Assembly,* That David Bullock, William C. Williams, and John Ambler, are hereby appointed commissioners for the purpose of renting a suitable house, and necessary out-houses, for the accommodation of the Governor of this Commonwealth for one year.

2. *And be it further enacted,* That the Commissioners aforesaid are hereby authorised and required to purchase suitable furniture for the said house; provided it does not exceed two thousand dollars: And the Auditor of Public Accounts is hereby authorised and required to issue his warrant in favor of the said Commissioners for the amount of expenses incurred by the purchase of the furniture aforesaid.

3. This act shall commence and be in force from and after the passing thereof.

Document 3. An Act appropriating a further sum
of money for the completion of the Governor's house,
and for other purposes. [Passed February 18, 1812.]

Whereas it appears by the report of the commissioners appointed by an act, "directing the sale of certain public property, and for other purposes," that the sum appropriated is not sufficient to complete the Governor's house;

1. *Be it enacted by the General Assembly,* That the auditor of public accounts be and he is hereby authorised and directed to issue his warrant in favour of the commissioners aforesaid for the sum of three thousand dollars, for the purpose of completing the Governor's house.

2. *And be it further enacted,* That the auditor of public accounts be and he is hereby authorised and directed to issue his warrant in favor of the commissioners aforesaid for the sum of five thousand dollars, for the purpose of erecting convenient and necessary out houses and enclosures to the Governor's house.

3. This act shall commence and be in force from and after the passing thereof.

Document 4. An Act appointing Commissioners to purchase
Furniture for the Governor's House. [Passed January 27, 1813.]

1. *Be it enacted by the General Assembly,* That David Bullock, William C. Williams, and John Ambler are hereby appointed commissioners for the purpose of purchasing additional furniture for the Governor's house.

2. *And be it further enacted,* That the commissioners aforesaid are hereby authorised and required to purchase suitable furniture for the house aforesaid in addition to that now appertaining to said house; provided that, it does not exceed the sum of three thousand dollars; and that the auditor of public accounts is hereby authorised and required to issue his warrant in favour of the said commissioners, or any two of them, for the amount of expenses incurred by the purchase of the furniture aforesaid.

3. This act shall commence and be in force from and after the passing thereof.

Document 5. Agreement with Tompkins, June 18, 1811

It is understood, and agreed upon, between The Commis. within named, and myself the Contractor, Christopher Tompkins, That all work done, and materials furnished by me, on, or for the building to be by me erected for the use of the Governor of this Commonwealth; And which are, or may not be particularly cited in the Estimate rendered, & Contract entered into by me with said Commis. are to be paid, & settled for by them at the same Rate, & price, the work &c &c therein mentioned is fixed at. And any work, or materials so Contracted to be done & provided which they the Commiss may think proper to dispense with. Due Credit at the rates & prices named in said Estimate &c shall be given by me therefor. Eighteenth of June Eighteen hundred & Eleven.

CHRISTOPHER TOMPKINS

Document 6. The Referees' Valuation and Report, February 9, 1813
Copy of the Referees Valuation, & Report.

Agreeable to appointment of 18th January 1813. By the Commissioners chosen to superintendent the public Work at the Governors House, on their part: and Christopher Tompkins (the Contractor) on his part; We the Subscribers, have measured & valued all the

Work, and Materials furnished by said Tompkins, Variant from Estimate including two porticoes put up at the End Doors of Dwelling House; And fifty Dollars paid Alex. Parriss for Drawing the plan of said Dwelling house: And find the Amount to be Two thousand, seven hundred, & eighty six Dollars & seven & half Cents; which Sum the said Tompkins is to receive, over, and Above the Sum of Eleven thousand, seven hundred, And Thirty nine Dollars & Forty five, & half Cents mentioned in said Tompkins Contract; Making in the whole the Sum of Fourteen thousand, five Hundred, and twenty five Dollars, & fifty three Cents, for the dwelling House. In addition to the above, We have also measured, and valued the Out Houses (Kitchen, Smoke house, & Necessary) as compleat, including the Enclosure. That is thirty Eight pannel of plank Fence, and nineteen pannels of pale Enclosure, round yard, as now Stands; Also adding the Sum of Eight hundred & seventeen Dollars, and fifty six Cents, paid by said Tompkins for digging & moving the Earth In levelling the Yard, Making the further Sum of Three thousand, nine Hundred, & eighty six Dollars & twenty nine Cents which added to the above will make the Whole aggregate amount to be Eighteen thousand, Five Hundred & Eleven Dollars, & Eighty two Cents.

As given under our hands this 9th Day of Feby. 1813.

ALEX. MCKIMM
WILSON BRYAN

Document 7. Report of the Commissioners

Virginia, City of Richmond, February 12, 1813.

Report of the Commissioners appointed by an act of Assembly, passed the 13th February A. D. 1811, entitled an act, directing the sale of certain public property, and for other purposes.

By virtue also, of one other act of Assembly, passed on the 18th February, A. D. 1812, entitled an act, appropriating a farther sum of money, for the completion of the Governor's house, and for other purposes.

They, the Commissioners acting under the aforesaid authority, and whose names are hereto subscribed, proceeded to take the same under consideration. And after mature deliberation, determined that, consulting as well the honor and dignity of the state, as the conveniency of the Chief Magistrate, who might, when completed, occupy the same; They would cause the principal story of said building to be finished off in a style rather superior to that originally contemplated; and to erect two plain porches on the north and south fronts of said building. This their determination, of course producing a deviation from the plan originally entered into with the undertaker, Christopher Tompkins; as well also, that a just and true estimate might be rendered, of such work, materials furnished, &c. by him, said undertaker; mutually agreed with him that all the work and materials by him the said Christopher Tompkins performed, and supplied variant from the contract originally entered into, should be in value fixed, determined and ascertained by the two disinterested and competent characters, Alexander McKim on the part of the commonwealth, and Wilson Bryan, on that of him the aforenamed undertaker. By their report, (which your honorable body will find herewith sent, under date of the 9th present,) it will be seen, that the actual cost of the dwelling house, for the use of the Chief Magistrate,

is fixed at	Dolls. 14525 53
Less than the sum therefor appropriated,	474 47
Whole sums by aforesaid two acts of General Assembly being,	Dolls. 15000 00

And that actual cost of all and every of the out houses, on said scite erected, together with the plank enclosure, digging and removal of a vast body of earth, as well to bring it to a more even surface, as to encrease its level extent by filling up the ravine:

Said mutually chosen referees fixed at,	Dolls. 3986 20
Less than the sum for this purpose granted,	1013 71
By act of Assembly appropriated,	Dolls. 5000 00
Remaining from this statement, first a balance of	Dolls. 474 47
And secondly of	1013 71
Which balance is chargeable with the	Dolls. 1488 18

Sum of 60 dollars due by account to their referee,
Alexander McKim, as compensation for valuing,
&c. And the further sum of 300 dollars to
William McKim, whose services the
commissioners thought it necessary to command,
during the years 1811 and 1812, for the
superintendancy, planning, &c. of the work
to be performed,   Dolls. 360 00

Leaving, after said deductions, an unexpended
balance of 1128 dollars 18 cents, a part of
which, will be necessarily consumed in
finishing the enclosure.   Dolls. 1128 18

Your Commissioners, with respectful deference to your honorable body, beg leave to observe, that the exterior view of the building, the comfort and conveniency of its habitants, would (in their opinion) be greatly encreased by the superstructure of a terrace surrounding the eaves of the building, and of a portico to the door fronting the Capitol; that to the fire places, marble hearths and slabs ought to be substituted for the plain (now standing) brick ones; that ornamental trees around the buildings would greatly improve the look and comfort of the lot; and further to compleat the tenement for the accommodation of the common-wealth's Chief Magistrate, they (with due deference) submit the propriety of purchasing, (if to be procured,) the private property, immediately south of the recently erected Chief Magistrate's dwelling house, adjoining F and 13th street. The circumjacent ravine filled up with the earth taken off to bring it to a level with the improved part of the lot, would afford ground sufficient for a garden, and the erection of a stable, carriage house, &c. which the decayed state of the one, now existing, renders it necessary to supply the place of.

Should the purchase of the small slip of ground, (in order to make the lot compleat,) be by your honorable body authorised, it would be necessary to open F street from 11th to 13th street, on which street, (thus opened,) a proper situation for the stable and carriage house would be found, as also a more eligible one for the temple [i.e., privy], than where it now stands.

All which is with due deference, respectfully submitted,

DAVID BULLOCK,
WM. M'KIM,
RO. GREENHOW.

Appendix C
Members of the Citizens Advisory Council for Interpreting and Furnishing the Executive Mansion, 1973-1988

Mrs. A. Smith Bowman
Sunset Hills 1973-78

Tennant Bryan
Richmond 1973-78

Mrs. George M. Cochran
Staunton 1973-79

Mrs. Richard Cutts
The Plains 1973-79

Mrs. George E. Flippen, Jr.
Lynchburg 1973-79

Dr. William H. Higgins, Jr.
Richmond 1973-76, 1978-81

Floyd Johnson
Charlottesville 1973-78

Mrs. George M. Kaufman
Norfolk 1973-76, 1978-81

Augustus C. Long
North 1973-78

Mrs. Charles Beatty Moore
Gloucester 1973-76, 1978

Mrs. Benjamin F. Parrott
Roanoke 1973-78

Frank W. Rogers, Jr.
Roanoke 1973-78

Mrs. George Rogers Clarke Stuart
Abingdon 1973-74

J. Harvie Wilkinson, Jr.
Richmond 1973-76

Mrs. William R. Aikens
Danville 1978-83

Edward L. Breeden, Jr.
Norfolk 1973-76, 1978-81

Mrs. Richard E. Byrd
Berryville 1973-76

Clement E. Conger
Alexandria 1973-76, 1978-81, 1982-86

Mrs. Leon Dure, Jr.
Charlottesville 1973-79

Mrs. Richmond Gray
Richmond 1973-76

Carlisle H. Humelsine
Williamsburg 1973-76, 1978-81

Mrs. J. Howard Joynt
Alexandria 1973-78

Mrs. B. B. Lane
Altavista 1973-78

Benjamin W. Mears
Eastville 1973-79

Mrs. W. Tayloe Murphy, Jr.
Montross 1973-78

Ms. Anne Dobie Peebles
Carson 1973-79

Mrs. William Reed III
Manakin-Sabot 1973-78

Mrs. Paul E. Sackett
Lynchburg 1973-79, 1983-85

Marcellus Wright, Jr.
Richmond 1974-79

James M. Blair
Vinton 1978-81

Mrs. Toy D. Savage, Jr.
Norfolk 1983–88

Mrs. Gayle Perkins Atkins
Alexandria 1984–89

Frank T. Eck
Richmond 1984–89

Mrs. Stanley E. Harrison
Vienna 1984–89

Porcher L. Taylor, Jr.
Petersburg 1984–89

Mrs. Peter Ward
Lynchburg 1985–88, 1988–93

Ronald L. Hurst
Williamsburg 1986–87

Susan Siegel
Manakin-Sabot 1986–91

Meredith N. Beal
Richmond 1988–93

William L. Beiswanger
Charlottesville 1988–93

Constance T. Bundy
Abingdon 1988–93

Elizabeth D. Darden
Norfolk 1988–93

Nancy Hand Hirst
McLean 1988–93

Sybil M. Walker
Norfolk 1988–93

Lynette Taylor
Alexandria 1983–88

Barbara E. Berry
Grundy 1984–89

Katherine Kennon Hamilton
Ashland 1984–89

Mrs. David Lay
Kilmarnock 1984–89

Mrs. Jack Trayer
Bristol 1984–89

Conover Hunt
Hampton 1986–87

Benjamin J. Levy
Virginia Beach 1986–91

John G. Zehmer, Jr.
Richmond 1986–91

Charles E. Brownell III
Midlothian 1988–91

Dr. Jessie Lemon Brown
Hampton 1988–93

Shirlie S. Camp
Franklin 1988–93

Roxann B. Dillon
Bassett 1988–93

Carolyn R. Pflug
Springfield 1988–93

Mary Louise B. Walker
Roanoke 1988–93

Bibliography

THREE major manuscript collections were used in the research for this book. All are in the Archives Branch of the Virginia State Library and Archives in Richmond. The first and most important is a large body of manuscript pages grouped under the title "Capitol Square Data, Records, 1784–1931" found in the papers of the auditor of public accounts. Part of this collection is excerpted in typescript, while the balance remains as it was originally written through the years. Here is found the day-to-day material pertaining to the Executive Mansion, from inventories to accounts of housepainters and carpenters, bricklayers and guards. The sources are richer for some areas than for others, but pertain mainly to the physical house and its surroundings on Capitol Square.

The Governor's Papers are the public and official papers of the executive. Once again these vary in fullness, but in general they are abundant. One must dig to find much there on the mansion, although some treasures do appear. Almost without exception, however, an investigation sends the scholar in search of the governors' private papers, which are often at the Virginia Historical Society or the Manuscripts Department of the University of Virginia. In the personal account books and letters, mention is made of the mansion not for official reasons but for private ones, for the house was, if only for a short time, the domicile of the governor in question. As problems of maintenance or use had to be addressed by the governor, inquiries and solutions slipped into his letters or accounts. Of more occasional use are the Land Office Records, where among the papers of the superintendent of public buildings some information was found about the first governor's houses and later the mansion.

Information on personalities and social life—as well as politics, insofar as that has concerned me—has come from a wide variety of books and articles. Below is a partial listing, compiled for two purposes, 1) to identify the writings that helped me the most in understanding the past of the mansion, and 2) to recommend those works, published and unpublished, that I found to be well written or especially informative. Few center directly on the mansion itself, but they touch on its characters and the eras through which it has lived. Anyone wanting to read more from the particular perspective I have followed will find great satisfaction in these historical works.

BOOKS

Ambler, Charles H. *Francis H. Pierpont: Union War Governor of Virginia and Father of West Virginia.* Chapel Hill: University of North Carolina Press, 1937.

———, ed. *The Life and Diary of John Floyd.* Richmond: Richmond Press, Inc., 1918.

Ammon, Harry. *James Monroe: The Quest for National Identity.* New York: McGraw-Hill Book Company, 1971.

Anderson, Dice Robins. *William Branch Giles: A Study in the Politics of Virginia and the Nation from 1790 to 1830.* Menasha, Wis.: George Banta Publishing Co., 1914.

Andrews, M. Carl. *No Higher Honor: The Story of Mills Godwin, Jr.* Richmond: Dietz Press, Inc., 1970.

Bass, Jack, and DeVries, Walter. *The Transformation of Southern Politics: Social Change and Political Consequence Since 1945.* New York: Basic Books, Inc., 1976.

Bell, John W. *Memoirs of Governor William Smith, of Virginia.* New York: Moss Engraving Company, 1891.

Bernard, George S., comp. and ed. *War Talks of Confederate Veterans.* Petersburg: Fenn & Owen, 1892.

Blackford, Charles Minor, III, ed. *Letters From Lee's Army.* New York: Charles Scribner's Sons, 1947.

Blake, Nelson Morehouse. *William Mahone of Virginia: Soldier and Political Insurgent.* Richmond: Garrett & Massie, 1935.

Blunt, Charles P., IV. *Patrick Henry: The Henry County Years (1779–1784).* Danville, Va.: Womack Press, 1976.

Boney, F. N. *John Letcher of Virginia: The Story of Virginia's Civil War Governor.* University, Ala.: University of Alabama Press, 1966.

Boyd, Thomas. *Light-Horse Harry Lee.* New York: Charles Scribner's Sons, 1931.

Bradshaw, Herbert Clarence. *History of Prince Edward County.* Richmond: Dietz Press, Inc., 1955.

Brock, R. A. *Virginia and Virginians: Eminent Virginians.* 2 vols. Richmond: H. H. Hardesty, Publisher, 1888.

Brown, Alexander. *The Cabells and Their Kin: A Memorial Volume.* Boston: Houghton, Mifflin, and Company, 1895. Reprint. Richmond: Garrett & Massie, Inc., 1939.

Buni, Andrew. *The Negro in Virginia Politics, 1902–1965.* Charlottesville: University Press of Virginia, 1967.

Caynor, Avis. *Bridgeport: The Town and Its People.* Bridgeport, W.Va.: Benedum Civic Center Library, 1976.

Chambers, Lenoir, and Shank, Joseph E. *Salt Water & Printer's Ink: Norfolk and Its Newspapers, 1865–1965.* Chapel Hill: University of North Carolina Press, 1967.

Chitwood, Oliver Perry. *John Tyler: Champion of the Old South.* New York: D. Appleton-Century Company, 1939.

Christian, W. Asbury. *Richmond: Her Past and Present.* Richmond: L. H. Jenkins, 1912.

Conway, Moncure Daniel. *Omitted Chapters of History Disclosed in the Life and Papers of Edmund Randolph.* New York: G. P. Putnam's Sons, 1888.

Crawley, William Bryan, Jr. *Bill Tuck: A Political Life in Harry Byrd's Virginia.* Charlottesville: University Press of Virginia, 1978.

Curry, Richard Orr. *A House Divided: A Study of Statehood Politics and the Copperhead Movement in West Virginia.* Pittsburgh: University of Pittsburgh Press, 1964.

Dabney, Virginius. *Dry Messiah: The Life of Bishop Cannon.* New York: Alfred A. Knopf, 1949.

———. *Richmond: The Story of a City.* Garden City, N.Y.: Doubleday & Company, Inc., 1976.

———. *Virginia: The New Dominion.* Garden City, N.Y.: Doubleday & Company, Inc., 1971.

Dalton, Edwina P. *The Virginia Executive Mansion.* [Richmond: n.p., ca. 1981].

Daniel, Jean Houston, and Daniel, Price. *Executive Mansions and Capitols of America.* Waukesha, Wis.: Country Beautiful, 1969.

Dumbauld, Edward. *Thomas Jefferson, American Tourist*. Norman: University of Oklahoma Press, 1946.

Eckenrode, Hamilton James. *The Political History of Virginia During the Reconstruction*. Johns Hopkins University Studies in Historical and Political Science, ser. 22, nos. 6-8. Baltimore: Johns Hopkins Press, 1904.

———. *The Randolphs: The Story of a Virginia Family*. New York: Bobbs-Merrill Company, 1946.

Eisenberg, Ralph. "Virginia: The Emergence of Two-Party Politics." In *The Changing Politics of the South,* edited by William C. Havard, 39-91. Baton Rouge: Louisiana State University Press, 1972.

Ely, James W., Jr. *The Crisis of Conservative Virginia: The Byrd Organization and the Politics of Massive Resistance*. Knoxville: University of Tennessee Press, 1976.

Fahrner, Alvin A. "William 'Extra Billy' Smith, Democratic Governor of Virginia, 1846-1849." In *Essays in Southern Biography,* 36-53. East Carolina College Publications in History, vol. 2. Greenville, N.C.: Department of History, East Carolina College, 1965.

Ferrell, Henry C., Jr. *Claude A. Swanson of Virginia: A Political Biography*. Lexington: University Press of Kentucky, 1985.

———. "Prohibition, Reform, and Politics in Virginia, 1895-1916." In *Studies in the History of the South, 1875-1922,* 175-242. East Carolina College Publications in History, vol. 3. Greenville, N.C.: Department of History, East Carolina College, 1966.

———. "The Role of Virginia Democratic Party Factionalism in the Rise of Harry Flood Byrd, 1917-1923." In *Essays in Southern Biography,* 146-166. East Carolina College Publications in History, vol. 2. Greenville, N.C.: Department of History, East Carolina College, 1965.

Flournoy, H. W. *Calendar of Virginia State Papers and Other Manuscripts From January 1, 1836, to April 15, 1869; Preserved in the Capitol at Richmond*. Vol. 11. Richmond: James E. Goode, Printer, 1893.

Freeman, Douglas Southall. *R. E. Lee: A Biography*. 4 vols. New York: Charles Scribner's Sons, 1934-1935.

———. *Lee's Lieutenants: A Study in Command*. 3 vols. New York: Charles Scribner's Sons, 1942-1944.

Fridell, Guy. *Colgate Darden: Conversations With Guy Fridell*. Charlottesville: University Press of Virginia, 1978.

Gaines, William H., Jr. *Thomas Mann Randolph: Jefferson's Son-in-Law*. Baton Rouge: Louisiana State University Press, 1966.

Gates, Robbins L. *The Making of Massive Resistance: Virginia's Politics of Public School Desegregation, 1954-1956*. Chapel Hill: University of North Carolina Press, 1964.

Gerson, Noel B. *Light-Horse Harry: A Biography of Washington's Great Cavalryman, General Henry Lee*. Garden City, N.Y.: Doubleday & Company, Inc., 1966.

Godwin, Katherine. *Living in a Legacy: Virginia's Executive Mansion*. Richmond: Virginia State Chamber of Commerce, 1977.

Goldman, Eric F. *The Crucial Decade—And After: America, 1945-1960*. New York: Vintage Books, 1960.

Goode, John. *Recollections of a Lifetime*. New York: Neale Publishing Company, 1906.

Grigsby, Hugh Blair. *Discourse on the Life and Character of the Hon. Littleton Waller Tazewell*. Norfolk: J. D. Ghiselin, Jun., 1860.

―――. *The Virginia Convention of 1829-30*. Richmond: Macfarlane & Fergusson, 1854. Reprint. New York: DeCapo Press, 1969.

Hancock, Elizabeth H., ed. *Autobiography of John E. Massey*. New York: Neale Publishing Company, 1909.

Harlan, Louis R. *Separate and Unequal: Public School Campaigns and Racism in the Southern Seaboard States, 1901-1915*. Chapel Hill: University of North Carolina Press, 1958.

Hatch, Alden. *The Byrds of Virginia*. New York: Holt, Rinehart, and Winston, 1969.

Henderson, William D. *The Unredeemed City: Reconstruction in Petersburg, Virginia, 1865-1874*. Washington, D.C.: University Press of America, 1977.

Hendrick, Burton J. *The Lees of Virginia: Biography of a Family*. Boston: Little, Brown, and Company, 1935.

Hood, Graham. Introduction to *An Inventory of the Contents of the Governor's Palace Taken After the Death of Lord Botetourt*. Williamsburg: Colonial Williamsburg Foundation, 1987.

Hunter, Robert M. "Virginia and the New Deal." In *The New Deal: The State and Local Levels,* 2 vols., edited by John Braeman, Robert H. Bremner, and David Brody, 2:103-136. Columbus: Ohio State University Press, 1975.

Jones, J. B. *A Rebel War Clerk's Diary at the Confederate States Capital*. 2 vols. Edited by Howard Swiggert. Philadelphia: J. B. Lippincott & Co., 1866. New and enl. ed. New York: Old Hickory Bookshop, 1935.

Ketcham, Ralph. *James Madison: A Biography*. New York: Macmillan Company, 1971.

Key, V. O., Jr. *Southern Politics in State and Nation*. New York: Alfred A. Knopf, 1949.

Kimball, Marie. *Jefferson: War and Peace, 1776 to 1784*. New York: Coward-McCann, Inc., 1947.

Kimmel, Stanley. *Mr. Davis's Richmond*. New York: Coward-McCann, Inc., 1958.

Kirby, Jack Temple. *Westmoreland Davis: Virginia Planter-Politician, 1859-1942*. Charlottesville: University Press of Virginia, 1968.

Kirker, Harold. *The Architecture of Charles Bulfinch*. Cambridge: Harvard University Press, 1969.

Kluger, Richard. *Simple Justice: The History of "Brown v. Board of Education" and Black America's Struggle for Equality*. New York: Alfred A. Knopf, 1976.

Langhorne, Orra. *Southern Sketches From Virginia, 1881-1901*. Edited by Charles E. Wynes. Charlottesville: University Press of Virginia, 1964.

Larson, William. *Montague of Virginia: The Making of a Southern Progressive*. Baton Rouge: Louisiana State University Press, 1965.

Lichtenstein, Gaston. *Thomas Jefferson As War Governor.* Richmond: William Byrd Press, 1925.

Little, John P. *History of Richmond.* Richmond: Macfarlane & Fergusson, 1851. Reprint. Richmond: Dietz Printing Company, 1933.

Lowery, Charles D. *James Barbour: A Jeffersonian Republican.* University, Ala.: University of Alabama Press, 1984.

Lutz, Earle. *A Richmond Album.* Richmond: Garrett & Massie, 1937.

McDaniel, Ralph Clipman. *The Virginia Constitutional Convention of 1901-1902.* Johns Hopkins University Studies in Historical and Political Science, ser. 46, no. 3. Baltimore: Johns Hopkins Press, 1928.

McDonough, James L. *Schofield: Union General in the Civil War and Reconstruction.* Tallahassee: Florida State University Press, 1972.

Macrae, David. *The Americans at Home.* New York: E. P. Dutton & Co., Inc., 1952.

Maddex, Jack P., Jr. *The Virginia Conservatives, 1867-1879: A Study in Reconstruction Politics.* Chapel Hill: University of North Carolina Press, 1970.

Malone, Dumas. *Jefferson the Virginian.* Vol. 1, *Jefferson and His Time.* Boston: Little, Brown & Co., 1948.

Mann, Etta Donnan. *Four Years in the Governor's Mansion of Virginia, 1910-1914.* Richmond: Dietz Press, 1937.

Meade, Robert Douthat. *Patrick Henry: Patriot in the Making.* Philadelphia: J. B. Lippincott Company, 1957.

Miller, Francis Pickens. *Man From the Valley: Memoirs of a 20th-Century Virginian.* Chapel Hill: University of North Carolina Press, 1971.

Miller, Sally Campbell Preston. "James McDowell." Sketch in *History of Washington College,* by William Henry Ruffner, 37-201. Washington and Lee University Historical Papers, vol. 5. Baltimore: John Murphy & Co., 1895.

Moger, Allen W. *Virginia: Bourbonism to Byrd, 1870-1925.* Charlottesville: University Press of Virginia, 1968.

Moore, James Tice. *Two Paths to the New South: The Virginia Debt Controversy, 1870-1883.* Lexington: University Press of Kentucky, 1974.

Mordecai, Samuel. *Richmond in By-Gone Days: Being Reminiscences of an Old Citizen.* Richmond: G. M. West, 1856. 2d ed. Richmond: West & Johnson, Publishers, 1860. Reprinted from 2d ed. Richmond: Dietz Press, Inc., 1946.

Munford, Beverley B. *Virginia's Attitude Toward Slavery and Secession.* New York: Longmans, Green, and Co., 1909.

Munford, Robert Beverley, Jr. *Richmond Homes and Memories.* Richmond: Garrett & Massie, Inc., 1936.

Muse, Benjamin. *Virginia's Massive Resistance.* Bloomington: Indiana University Press, 1961.

O'Ferrall, Charles T. *Forty Years of Active Service.* New York: Neale Publishing Company, 1904.

Pearson, Charles Chilton. *The Readjuster Movement in Virginia.* New Haven: Yale University Press, 1917.

Peterson, Norma Lois. *Littleton Waller Tazewell.* Charlottesville: University Press of Virginia, 1983.

Pollard, Julia Cuthbert. *Richmond's Story.* Richmond: Richmond Public Schools, 1954.

Pulley, Raymond H. *Old Virginia Restored: An Interpretation of the Progressive Impulse, 1870–1930.* Charlottesville: University Press of Virginia, 1968.

Putnam, Sallie A. Brock. *Richmond During the War: Four Years of Personal Observation.* New York: G. W. Carleton & Co., Publishers, 1867.

Ruffner, William Henry. "James McDowell." Sketch in *History of Washington College*, 128–134. Washington and Lee University Historical Papers, vol. 4. Baltimore: John Murphy & Co., 1893.

Sabato, Larry. *Aftermath of "Armageddon": An Analysis of the 1973 Virginia Gubernatorial Election.* Institute of Government, University of Virginia. Charlottesville: University Printing Office, 1975.

Schlegel, Marvin W. *Conscripted City: Norfolk in World War II.* Norfolk: Norfolk War History Commission, 1951.

———. *Virginia on Guard: Civilian Defense and the State Militia in the Second World War.* Richmond: Virginia State Library, 1949.

Schofield, Lieutenant-General John M. *Forty-six Years in the Army.* New York: Century Co., 1897.

Sheldon, William DuBose. *Populism in the Old Dominion: Virginia Farm Politics, 1885–1900.* Princeton: Princeton University Press, 1935.

Simpson, Craig M. *A Good Southerner: The Life of Henry A. Wise of Virginia.* Chapel Hill: University of North Carolina Press, 1985.

Siviter, Anna Pierpont. *Recollections of War and Peace, 1861–1868.* Edited by Charles H. Ambler. New York: G. P. Putnam's Sons, 1938.

Smith, Margaret Vowell. *Virginia, 1492–1892: A Brief Review of the Discovery of the Continent of North America with a History of the Executives of the Colony and of the Commonwealth of Virginia, in Two Parts.* Washington, D.C.: W. H. Lowdermilk & Co., 1893.

Smith, Bob. *They Closed Their Schools: Prince Edward County, Virginia, 1951–1964.* Chapel Hill: University of North Carolina Press, 1965.

Stanard, Mary Newton. *Richmond: Its People and Its Story.* Philadelphia: J. B. Lippincott Company, 1923.

Stuart, Alexander H. H. *A Narrative of the Leading Incidents of the Organization of the First Popular Movement in Virginia in 1865. . . .* Richmond: Wm. Ellis Jones, Book and Job Printer, 1888.

Squires, W. H. T. *Through Centuries Three: A Short History of the People of Virginia.* Portsmouth, Va.: Printcraft Press, 1929.

Tyler, Lyon G. *The Letters and Times of the Tylers.* 3 vols. Richmond: Whittet & Shepperson, 1884–1885; Williamsburg: n.p., 1896.

Wilkinson, J. Harvie, III. *Harry Byrd and the Changing Face of Virginia Politics, 1945–1966.* Charlottesville: University Press of Virginia, 1968.

Willison, George F. *Patrick Henry and His World.* Garden City, N.Y.: Doubleday and Company, Inc., 1969.

Wise, Barton H. *The Life of Henry A. Wise of Virginia, 1806–1876.* New York: Macmillan Company, 1899.

Wise, John S. *The End of an Era.* Edited by Curtis Carroll Davis. Boston: Houghton, Mifflin, and Company, 1899. New ed. New York: Thomas Yoseloff, 1965.

Wynes, Charles E. *Race Relations in Virginia, 1870–1902.* Charlottesville: University Press of Virginia, 1961.

Younger, Edward; Moore, James Tice; et al., eds. *The Governors of Virginia, 1860–1978.* Charlottesville: University Press of Virginia, 1982.

ARTICLES

Alexander, Robert L. "Maximilian Godefroy in Virginia: A French Interlude in Richmond's Architecture." *Virginia Magazine of History and Biography* 69 (1961): 419–431.

Bolinaga, Shirley. "The Happy Governor." *Commonwealth* 37 (August 1970): 23–27.

Byrd, Harry F. "Virginia Through the Eyes of Her Governor." *Scribner's Magazine* 83 (1928): 682–689.

Chesson, Michael B. "Harlots or Heroines? A New Look at the Richmond Bread Riot." *Virginia Magazine of History and Biography* 92 (1984): 131–175.

Dabney, Virginius. "American We Like: Governor Byrd of Virginia." *Nation* 126 (1928): 632–634.

Daffron, John F. "Calm John Battle Was Never Rattled." *Commonwealth* 21 (February 1954): 17–18.

Dimmock, Charles. "Putting George on a Pedestal." *Richmond Times-Dispatch*, magazine section, February 24, 1935.

Eggleston, J. D., Jr. "Claude Swanson—A Sketch." *Virginia Journal of Education* 1 (October 1907): 1–5.

Ethridge, Harrison M. "The Jordan Hatcher Affair of 1852: Cold Justice and Warm Compassion." *Virginia Magazine of History and Biography* 84 (1976): 446–463.

Fahrner, Alvin A. "William 'Extra Billy' Smith, Governor of Virginia, 1864–1865: A Pillar of the Confederacy." *Virginia Magazine of History and Biography* 74 (1966): 68–87.

Fry, Joseph A. "The Organization in Control: George Campbell Peery, Governor of Virginia, 1934–1938." *Virginia Magazine of History and Biography* 82 (1974): 306–330.

Gaines, William H., Jr. "The Connecting Link: The Expansion of Virginia's Public High Schools, 1900–1910." *Virginia Cavalcade* 5 (Winter 1955): 15–19.

Gatewood, Joanne L. "Richmond During the Virginia Constitutional Convention of 1829–1830." *Virginia Magazine of History and Biography* 84 (1976): 287–332.

Hall, Alvin L. "Virginia Back in the Fold: The Gubernatorial Campaign and Election of 1929." *Virginia Magazine of History and Biography* 73 (1965): 280–302.

Hathorn, Guy B. "Congressional Campaign in the Fighting Ninth: The Contest Between C. Bascom Slemp and Henry C. Stuart." *Virginia Magazine of History and Biography* 66 (1958): 337–344.

Henriques, Peter R. "The Organization Challenged: John S. Battle, Francis P. Miller, and Horace Edwards Run for Governor in 1949." *Virginia Magazine of History and Biography* 82 (1974): 372–406.

Hill, Don. "67th Governor of the Commonwealth of Virginia: Linwood Holton, Jr." *Virginia Record* 92 (January 1970): 8–16, 113–116.

Hohner, Robert A. "Prohibition and Virginia Politics: William Hodges Mann Versus Henry St. George Tucker, 1909." *Virginia Magazine of History and Biography* 74 (1966): 88–107.

Hutton, James V., Jr. "The One-Armed Hero of the Shenandoah." *Virginia Cavalcade* 19 (Summer 1969): 4–11.

Jones, Robert R. "James L. Kemper and the Virginia Redeemers Face the Race Question: A Reconsideration." *Journal of Southern History* 38 (1972): 393–414.

Keezell, George B. "History of the Establishment of the State Teachers College at Harrisonburg." *Virginia Teacher* 9 (1928): 133–146.

Lowance, Carter O. "The Governor of Virginia." *University of Virginia News Letter* 36 (1959–1960): 21–24.

McDowell, Charles, Jr. "J. Lindsay Almond, Jr.: New Virginia Governor Excels as an Orator." *Commonwealth* 25 (January 1958): 9–10.

Meade, Robert Douthat. "Judge Edmund Winston's Memoir of Patrick Henry." *Virginia Magazine of History and Biography* 69 (1961): 28–41.

Monkhouse, Christopher. "Parris Perusal." *Old Time New England* 58 (Fall 1967): 51–59.

O'Ferrall, Charles T. "Election Contest—Noyes vs. Rockwell . . . Speech of Hon. Charles T. O'Ferrall of Virginia, in the House of Representatives, Friday, April 22, 1892." *Appendix to Congressional Record*, 52d Cong., 1st sess., 1892. Vol. 23, pt. 8, pp. 234–243. Washington, D.C., 1892.

———. "The Nineteenth of January: Lee's Birth-Day." *Southern Historical Society Papers* 19 (1891): 402–405.

———. "O'Ferrall vs. Paul: Papers and Testimony in the Contested Election Case of C. T. O'Ferrall vs. John Paul, From the Seventh Congressional District of Virginia." *House Miscellaneous Document No. 16*, 48th Cong., 1st sess., vol. 8 (2220). Washington, D.C., 1884.

Smith, Anne Brooke. "Profile: Governor William 'Extra Billy' Smith." *Fauquier Historical Society News and Notes* 8 (Fall 1986): 1–5.

Taylor, Robert T. "The Jamestown Tercentennial Exposition of 1907." *Virginia Magazine of History and Biography* 65 (1957): 169–208.

Wooldridge, William C. "The Sound and Fury of 1896: Virginia Democrats Face Free Silver." *Virginia Magazine of History and Biography* 75 (1967): 97–108.

Wynes, Charles E. "Charles T. O'Ferrall and the Virginia Gubernatorial Election of 1893." *Virginia Magazine of History and Biography* 64 (1956): 437–453.

Zehmer, John G., Jr., and Driggs, Sarah Shields. " 'Worthy of Its Purposes': The Changing Face of the Governor's Mansion." *Virginia Cavalcade* 37 (1988): 126–133.

UNPUBLISHED MATERIALS

Atkins, Paul A. "Henry A. Wise and the Virginia Secession Convention, February 13–April 17, 1861." Master's thesis, University of Virginia, 1950.

Blanton, S. Walker, Jr. "Virginia in the 1920's: An Economic and Social Profile." Ph.D. diss., University of Virginia, 1969.

Bear, James A., Jr. "Thomas Staples Martin: A Study in Virginia Politics, 1883–1896." Master's thesis, University of Virginia, 1952.

Boudreau, Richard J. "Two-Party Politics in Virginia, 1888–1896." Master's thesis, University of Virginia, 1974.

Bristow, William Orlando, Jr. "The Political Career of Edmund Randolph." Master's thesis, University of Virginia, 1931.

Cahill, Audrey Marie. "Gilbert Carlton Walker: Virginia's Redeemer Governor." Master's thesis, University of Virginia, 1956.

Campbell, Otho C. "John Sergeant Wise: A Case Study in Conservative-Readjuster Politics in Virginia, 1869–1889." Ph.D. diss., University of Virginia, 1979.

Coyner, M. Boyd, Jr. "Thomas Walker Gilmer, 1802–1836: Origins of a Virginia Whig." Master's thesis, University of Virginia, 1954.

Crawley, William Bryan, Jr. "The Governorship of William M. Tuck, 1946–1950: Virginia Politics in the 'Golden Age' of the Byrd Organization." Ph.D. diss., University of Virginia, 1974.

Doss, Richard B. "John Warwick Daniel: A Study in the Virginia Democracy." Ph.D. diss., University of Virginia, 1955.

Driggs, Sarah S. "Workmen in Richmond, 1810–1835." Typescript, Historic Richmond Foundation, 1987.

Dunn, Isabel B. "The Executive Mansion, Richmond, Virginia." Typescript, Virginia State Library and Archives, December 1945.

Ely, James W., Jr. "The Crisis of Conservative Virginia: The Decline and Fall of Massive Resistance, 1957–1965." Ph.D. diss., University of Virginia, 1971.

Evans, Emory G. "The Nelsons: A Biographical Study of a Virginia Family in the Eighteenth-Century." Ph.D. diss., University of Virginia, 1957.

Fahrner, Alvin A. "The Public Career of William 'Extra Billy' Smith." Ph.D. diss., University of North Carolina, 1953.

Ferrell, Henry Clifton, Jr. "Claude A. Swanson of Virginia." Ph.D. diss., University of Virginia, 1964.

Fry, Joseph A. "George Campbell Peery: Conservative Son of Old Virginia." Master's thesis, University of Virginia, 1970.

Gaines, Francis Pendleton, Jr. "The Political Career of James McDowell, 1830–1851." Master's thesis, University of Virginia, 1947.

———. "The Virginia Constitutional Convention of 1850-1851: A Study in Sectionalism." Ph.D. diss., University of Virginia, 1950.

Gay, Thomas Edward, Jr. "The Life and Political Career of J. Hoge Tyler, Governor of Virginia, 1898-1902." Ph.D. diss., University of Virginia, 1969.

Golladay, Victor Dennis. "The Nicholas Family of Virginia, 1722-1820." Ph.D. diss., University of Virginia, 1973.

Hall, Alvin L. "James H. Price and Virginia Politics, 1878-1943." Ph.D. diss., University of Virginia, 1970.

Hawkes, Robert T., Jr. "The Career of Harry Flood Byrd, Sr., to 1933." Ph.D. diss., University of Virginia, 1975.

———. "The Political Apprenticeship and Gubernatorial Term of Harry Flood Byrd." Master's thesis, University of Virginia, 1967.

Hege, Elma Josephine. "Benjamin Harrison and the American Revolution." Master's thesis, University of Virginia, 1939.

Heinemann, Ronald L. "Depression and New Deal in Virginia." Ph.D. diss., University of Virginia, 1968.

Henriques, Peter Ros. "John S. Battle and Virginia Politics, 1948-1953." Ph.D. diss., University of Virginia, 1971.

Hohner, Robert A. "Prohibition and Virginia Politics, 1900-1916." Ph.D. diss., Duke University, 1965.

Hopewell, John S. "An Outsider Looking In: John Garland Pollard and Machine Politics in Twentieth Century Virginia." Ph.D. diss., University of Virginia, 1976.

Jones, Robert R. "Conservative Virginian: The Post-War Career of Governor James Lawson Kemper." Ph.D. diss., University of Virginia, 1964.

———. "Forgotten Virginian: The Early Life and Career of James Lawson Kemper, 1823-1865." Master's thesis, University of Virginia, 1961.

Kaufman, Burton I. "Henry DeLaWarr Flood: A Case Study of Organization Politics in an Era of Reform." Ph.D. diss., Rice University, 1966.

Lowe, Richard Grady. "Republicans, Rebellion, and Reconstruction: The Republican Party in Virginia, 1856-1870." Ph.D. diss., University of Virginia, 1968.

Middleton, A. P. "Patrick Henry in the Governor's Palace." Memorandum, Colonial Williamsburg Foundation, Williamsburg, 1950.

Ours, Robert Maurice. "Virginia's First Redeemer Legislature, 1869-1871." Master's thesis, University of Virginia, 1966.

Porter, Julian P., Jr. "Frederick William Mackey Holliday, Governor of Virginia, 1878-1881." Master's thesis, University of Virginia, 1969.

Poston, Charles E. "Henry Carter Stuart in Virginia Politics, 1855-1933." Master's thesis, University of Virginia, 1970.

Readnour, Harry W. "General Fitzhugh Lee, 1835-1905: A Biographical Study." Ph.D. diss., University of Virginia, 1971.

Rhodes, William A. "The Administration of William Hodges Mann, Governor of Virginia, 1910-1914." Master's thesis, University of Virginia, 1968.

Riggan, Warren. "A Political Biography of Thomas Bahnson Stanley." Master's thesis, University of Richmond, 1965.

Rosenthal, Herbert Hillel. "James Barbour, Virginia Politician, 1775-1842." Master's thesis, University of Virginia, 1942.

Shibley, Ronald E. "G. Walter Mapp: Politics and Prohibition in Virginia, 1873-1941." Master's thesis, University of Virginia, 1966.

Smith, James Douglas. "Virginia during Reconstruction, 1865-1870: A Political, Economic and Social Study." Ph.D. diss., University of Virginia, 1960.

Smith, Leslie Winston. "Richmond During Presidential Reconstruction, 1865-1867." Ph.D. diss., University of Virginia, 1974.

Sweeney, James R. "Byrd and Anti-Byrd: The Struggle for Political Supremacy in Virginia, 1945-1954." Ph.D. diss., University of Notre Dame, 1973.

Tarter, Joe Brent. "Freshman Senator Harry F. Byrd, 1933-1934." Master's thesis, University of Virginia, 1972.

Teeter, Sara Etheredge. "Benjamin Harrison, Governor of Virginia, 1781-1784." Master's thesis, University of Richmond, 1965.

Templin, Thomas E. "Light Horse Harry Lee, Federalist." Master's thesis, University of Virginia, 1967.

Toombs, Kenneth E. "The Early Life of Littleton Waller Tazewell, 1774-1815." Master's thesis, University of Virginia, 1955.

Weeder, Elinor Janet. "Wilson Cary Nicholas, Jefferson's Lieutenant." Master's thesis, University of Virginia, 1946.

Weston, Elizabeth. "The Early Career of James Monroe." Master's thesis, University of Virginia, 1941.

White, Stephen Jennings. "The Partisan Political Element in the Virginia Constitutional Convention of 1850-1851." Master's thesis, University of Virginia, 1981.

Willis, Leo Stanley. "E. Lee Trinkle and the Virginia Democracy, 1876-1939." Ph.D. diss., University of Virginia, 1968.

———. "The Gubernatorial Administration of E. Lee Trinkle: Transition Years in the Life of Virginia's Democratic Organization." Master's thesis, University of Virginia, 1966.

Wolfe, Jonathan J. "Virginia in World War II." Ph.D. diss., University of Virginia, 1971.

Wyrick, Connie H. "The Executive Mansion of Virginia." Report for the Citizens Advisory Council on Furnishing and Interpreting the Executive Mansion, 2 vols., Richmond, April 1973.

Zimmer, Edward Francis. "The Architectural Career of Alexander Parris (1780-1852)." Ph.D. diss., Boston University, 1984.

Zuckerman, Bernice Bryant. "Philip Watkins McKinney, Governor of Virginia, 1890-1894." Master's thesis, University of Virginia, 1967.

Index

Virginia's Executive Mansion: A History of the Governor's House
was designed by Ronnie Sampson, of Richmond, set in Baskerville by
Typographics, Inc., of Richmond, and printed by
the John D. Lucas Printing Company, of Baltimore.
Commissioned color photography was by Erik Kvalsvik, of Baltimore.
At the Virginia State Library and Archives: copy photography was by
Mark H. Rainer; illustration and caption research was by Sarah Driggs;
editorial coordination was by Jon Kukla, Emily J. Salmon, and Sarah Driggs;
the index was prepared by Sandra Gioia Treadway and Donald W. Gunter;
and production coordination was by W. Donald Rhinesmith.